CHOOSE *You*

A GUIDED SELF–CARE JOURNAL
MADE *Just* FOR *You!*

SARA ROBINSON, MA

ADAMS MEDIA

NEW YORK   LONDON   TORONTO   SYDNEY   NEW DELHI

I have so much gratitude for Jackie Musser and Adams Media/Simon & Schuster for welcoming me into the family for this project. A big thank-you goes out to the women who shared their self-care experiences and activities—this journal is better because of you. And a huge thank-you to the gentlemen in my life who rally behind every project I take on, making sure I get the time (and the self-care) I need to get it all done well. B, E, and N—I love you!

A adamsmedia

Adams Media
An Imprint of Simon & Schuster, Inc.
57 Littlefield Street
Avon, Massachusetts 02322

First Adams Media trade paperback edition November 2018

ADAMS MEDIA and colophon are trademarks of Simon & Schuster.

For information about special discounts for bulk purchases, please contact Simon & Schuster Special Sales at 1-866-506-1949 or business@simonandschuster.com.

The Simon & Schuster Speakers Bureau can bring authors to your live event. For more information or to book an event contact the Simon & Schuster Speakers Bureau at 1-866-248-3049 or visit our website at www.simonspeakers.com.

Interior design by Katrina Machado
Interior images © Getty Images/grivina, kaylabutler, calvindexter, MariaArefyeva

Manufactured in the United States of America

10 9 8 7 6 5 4 3 2 1

Library of Congress Cataloging-in-Publication Data has been applied for.

ISBN 978-1-5072-0910-3

INTRODUCTION

Finding time that's just for you can seem tough, but you've decided to put yourself first! Congratulations for deciding to choose you!

But now that you've made this choice, you may find yourself wondering what to do next. Well, when it comes right down to it, the goal is to add more self-care into your life—in any way that you can! And self-care doesn't have to be just getting a mani-pedi or scheduling a spa day. Self-care can be whatever *you* want it to be, and this journal will help you figure out what works for your body, mind, and spirit—and why.

Here you'll find more than eighty journal entries that are full of feel-good self-care activities, words of encouragement that help you keep going, and quotes to help you stay inspired. You'll also find space to track your self-care activities as you figure out what routines work best for you. Finding the right self-care activities can be a bit of trial and error, so feel free to try new things! Have fun! Your choices are nearly unlimited, so if you try something you don't like, just note that you don't want to try it again in the "Today's Takeaway!" sections. Or, if you find something you love, write that down too. You want to be able to remember exactly what you did and how it made you feel so you can do it again!

And if you want to know more about self-care and how to make it easy, the following section gives you the basics of what you need to know, including how to find the time for self-care and the six key types of self-care that you may want to try.

Now is the time to *choose you*—so go ahead and make self-care a reality. Have fun!

All about Self-Care

If you're going to start adding more self-care into your life, it's important that you take a few minutes to learn a little more about this practice in general. After all, if you're going to benefit, you need to know what you're doing (or not doing!) in order to get the most out of the time you'll be putting in.

So what is self-care, anyway? How will it benefit you? How can you fit self-care into *your* busy schedule? You'll learn all this and more in this section. Let's get started!

What Is Self-Care?

Self-care, at its core, is simple—which is important because there are enough things in life that are complicated. It is acknowledging that *you* matter: that your well-being, mood, energy, and thoughts are priorities and not afterthoughts. It is taking care of yourself—body, mind, and spirit—and doing things that help you feel good. Actually, better than good. Self-care should help you feel great!

Think back to a time when you felt great. During that time, what were you doing to take care of yourself? How often did you put yourself first? Chances are that you were engaging in self-care, and you might not have even realized it! You likely had activities and routines that were important to you and helped you feel your best; choosing you was a consistent choice. Life can always be like that: you just have to prioritize yourself even—or especially!—when life is busy, stressful, or mundane.

So what can you do to practice self-care? Well, self-care comes in many different shapes and sizes; it's not one size fits all. As you'll see as you work through the different activities suggested in the "Feel-Good Ideas!" sections of the journal, what is considered self-care is unique to you. What this means is that it's important to find self-care activities that meet *your* needs and fit *your* available time. Maybe your friend thinks of spa days, alone time, or yoga as self-care. While these activities *are* self-care, they may not be *your* self-care. As you figure out what works for you, just keep in mind that almost anything can be a form of self-care—if it's done with mindfulness and intention!

The Six Types of Self-Care

While the self-care activities you choose to do are completely up to you, there are six types of self-care that you must focus on to fulfill your different fundamental needs. And when you engage in self-care activities that address these various needs, you can create a stronger sense of well-being, have more positive thoughts and feelings, and be more present in your everyday life. As you read about these different types of self-care, think about which areas feel like ones that you want to devote time and energy to.

☐ **EMOTIONAL SELF-CARE** includes taking time for your emotions or doing pleasurable activities, such as talking with a friend, watching a funny movie, dancing, or going to therapy. You need to take care of your emotions so you can experience positive feelings more often and more strongly than negative ones, and so you're prepared to handle the emotional challenges that life throws at you.

☐ **MENTAL SELF-CARE** is doing something mentally stimulating, such as playing a game, doing a puzzle, or doing something that allows you to take care of your mental state, like using affirmations or practicing kindness to yourself. Mentally, you need to keep your mind stimulated, engaged, and in a positive place so you can handle your day-to-day tasks with ease, confidence, and less mental stress.

- ☐ **PHYSICAL SELF-CARE** is taking care of your body and might include activities like exercise, eating well, stretching, or yoga. When you take care of yourself physically, you ensure that you stay healthy and have the energy to complete your daily tasks.
- ☐ **PRACTICAL SELF-CARE** is typically about what you need to do in a more logistical sense, such as decluttering, tackling something on your to-do list, or making doctors' appointments. When you complete these daily self-care activities and tasks that are more practical in nature, you may feel calmer, in control, satisfied, and accomplished.
- ☐ **SOCIAL SELF-CARE** uses friends and other people to help you maintain relationships, feel connected to others, and take care of yourself! This includes engaging in activities that include others or allow you to be social, like a night out with friends, a date night, or talking on the phone. When you have these needs met, you'll likely feel happier, more secure, and loved.
- ☐ **SPIRITUAL SELF-CARE** will depend on your spiritual beliefs but might include meditation, going to church, or praying. When you practice spiritual self-care, you feel more connected to a higher power and, therefore, more grounded and secure.

As you go through the journal, you'll find many activities to try that meet these various needs, or you can find another activity that works better for you! On each journal page, there's a spot for you to keep track of what type of self-care you decided to do, so just mark it off and see what types fit best into your life. And keep in mind that one activity can check off more than one of these types of self-care!

How Can You Find Time for Self-Care?

You're busy. That's 100 percent true. But you do have time for self-care—guaranteed!

One way you can find more time to choose you is to redefine what you consider to be self-care. Yes, spa days and weekends away are fantastic, but sometimes self-care is just taking five minutes in a quiet space to sit, breathe, and clear your mind.

Setting the right intention can turn a seemingly basic task into an important part of your routine. For example, maybe you have a morning cup of coffee that you drink quickly as you're rushing to get out of the house. If you make a small change and decide to get up ten minutes earlier to enjoy your coffee at a slower pace (and maybe with a book), this is now self-care! You're meeting your mental and emotional needs with this new morning routine—and maybe your physical needs, too, because that caffeine will help get you going!

Self-care also becomes easier when you make time for it in your schedule. Yes, plans change, but if you make time for the self-care activities that are important to you by scheduling them into your day and week, you give yourself a much better chance of following through. Look ahead at your week and find the places where you can plan time for yourself. It's also helpful to have a few quick activities that you can regularly do at the start or end of your day, such as sitting in silence for a few minutes, breathing deeply, listening to a song to feed your soul, or focusing on what you're grateful for. This way you get in at least a bit of self-care every day, no matter what else is going on.

Keep in mind that money should not be a barrier to self-care. You don't need to take the time to save up money in order to choose you! The focus is on taking care of yourself, and what you do does not have to be fancy or expensive. You can make self-care happen now, no matter what!

Get Ready to Choose You!

So now that you know how to choose you, it's time to give self-care a try! On each page in the journal, you'll find questions to answer about your day and your experience with the self-care activity you chose. You'll also reflect on how you were feeling before, during, and after your self-care, and you'll make note of what you enjoyed (or didn't), what type of self-care you did, and how it helped you. You'll even find a spot to add any and all notes that you want to remember about that self-care activity. Make your journal even more awesome by making sure each entry is all about you!

Remember that the journal prompts stay the same throughout the book, but don't forget to pay special attention to the extra information included! You'll find either a feel-good activity to try, an encouraging note that will help you keep things going in the right direction, or an inspiring quote that will keep you motivated. You may want to read through the prompts on each page all in one sitting and then read them again one at a time when you start a new journal page.

The feel-good activities included on the journal pages are meant to inspire you! You might want to do the activity as described, you may feel an adjustment is necessary, or you might decide that the activity is not for you. Some of the suggested activities will require planning, like a night out with friends. Even if it takes months to get this on the calendar, take the time to do it!

Lastly, don't be too hard on yourself as you practice self-care. Do your best to make yourself a priority, but don't feel guilty if you miss a day. The more you practice, the more you'll experience self-care's benefits. And as you use your journal to figure out what types of self-care work best for you and make you feel your best, chances are that you'll get even better at creating more time for them in your life.

Remember to always choose you; you're worth it!

Date: ....

Today's self-care activity: ....

....

....

....

....

....

....

☐ MAKE THIS A REGULAR ACTIVITY

☐ THIS IS GREAT FOR SPECIAL OCCASIONS

☐ GIVE THIS ANOTHER TRY ON A DIFFERENT DAY

☐ THIS ISN'T FOR ME

Choose You check-in...How did I feel?

BEFORE:	DURING:	AFTER:
☐ CALM	☐ RELAXED	☐ HOPEFUL
☐ CHEERFUL	☐ AWESOME	☐ CONFIDENT
☐ IN CONTROL	☐ STRONG	☐ PROUD
☐ STRESSED	☐ ENERGIZED	☐ PEACEFUL
☐ DISTRACTED	☐ HAPPY	☐ GROUNDED
☐ EMOTIONAL	☐ SURPRISED	☐ FOCUSED
☐ OVERWHELMED	☐ RELIEVED	☐ CONTENT
☐ ANXIOUS	☐ FREE	☐ _____
☐ ANGRY	☐ _____	☐ _____
☐ _____	☐ _____	☐ _____
☐ _____	☐ _____	☐ _____

THIS WAS JUST WHAT I NEEDED BECAUSE...

....

....

....

....

....

....

....

....

....

FEEL–GOOD IDEAS!

Get a new book you're excited to read and put it in your car or purse. When you find yourself waiting, take it out and start reading! You now have something meaningful to fill your time, and you can fit in short moments of mental self-care more easily.

MY AWESOME NOTES!

....

....

....

....

....

....

....

....

....

....

....

....

TODAY I CHOSE THIS TYPE OF SELF–CARE:

☐ EMOTIONAL

☐ MENTAL

☐ PHYSICAL

☐ PRACTICAL

☐ SOCIAL

☐ SPIRITUAL

DATE: ....

TODAY'S SELF—CARE ACTIVITY: ....

....

....

....

....

....

....

....

CHOOSE YOU CHECK-IN...HOW DID I FEEL?

BEFORE:

- ☐ CALM
- ☐ CHEERFUL
- ☐ IN CONTROL
- ☐ STRESSED
- ☐ DISTRACTED
- ☐ EMOTIONAL
- ☐ OVERWHELMED
- ☐ ANXIOUS
- ☐ ANGRY
- ☐ _____
- ☐ _____

DURING:

- ☐ RELAXED
- ☐ AWESOME
- ☐ STRONG
- ☐ ENERGIZED
- ☐ HAPPY
- ☐ SURPRISED
- ☐ RELIEVED
- ☐ FREE
- ☐ _____
- ☐ _____
- ☐ _____

AFTER:

- ☐ HOPEFUL
- ☐ CONFIDENT
- ☐ PROUD
- ☐ PEACEFUL
- ☐ GROUNDED
- ☐ FOCUSED
- ☐ CONTENT
- ☐ _____
- ☐ _____
- ☐ _____

THIS WAS JUST WHAT I NEEDED BECAUSE...

....

....

....

....

....

....

....

....

KEEP IT GOING!

Your frame of mind will influence your self-care habits, so change your inner dialogue to include positive thoughts about self-care! By thinking things like "I have enough time for self-care" or "These tasks are important," you're more likely to make the time and space you need to choose you.

MY AWESOME NOTES!

....

....

....

....

....

....

....

....

....

....

....

TODAY I CHOSE THIS TYPE OF SELF-CARE:

☐ EMOTIONAL

☐ MENTAL

☐ PHYSICAL

☐ PRACTICAL

☐ SOCIAL

☐ SPIRITUAL

DATE:

TODAY'S SELF-CARE ACTIVITY:

☐ MAKE THIS A REGULAR ACTIVITY

☐ THIS IS GREAT FOR SPECIAL OCCASIONS

☐ GIVE THIS ANOTHER TRY ON A DIFFERENT DAY

☐ THIS ISN'T FOR ME

CHOOSE YOU CHECK-IN... HOW DID I FEEL?

BEFORE:	DURING:	AFTER:
☐ CALM	☐ RELAXED	☐ HOPEFUL
☐ CHEERFUL	☐ AWESOME	☐ CONFIDENT
☐ IN CONTROL	☐ STRONG	☐ PROUD
☐ STRESSED	☐ ENERGIZED	☐ PEACEFUL
☐ DISTRACTED	☐ HAPPY	☐ GROUNDED
☐ EMOTIONAL	☐ SURPRISED	☐ FOCUSED
☐ OVERWHELMED	☐ RELIEVED	☐ CONTENT
☐ ANXIOUS	☐ FREE	☐ _____
☐ ANGRY	☐ _____	☐ _____
☐ _____	☐ _____	☐ _____
☐ _____	☐ _____	☐ _____

THIS WAS JUST WHAT I NEEDED BECAUSE...

....

....

....

....

....

....

....

....

....

MY AWESOME NOTES!

....

....

....

....

....

....

....

....

....

....

TODAY I CHOSE THIS TYPE OF SELF-CARE:

☐ EMOTIONAL

☐ MENTAL

☐ PHYSICAL

☐ PRACTICAL

☐ SOCIAL

☐ SPIRITUAL

DATE:

TODAY'S SELF—CARE ACTIVITY:

- ☐ MAKE THIS A REGULAR ACTIVITY
- ☐ THIS IS GREAT FOR SPECIAL OCCASIONS
- ☐ GIVE THIS ANOTHER TRY ON A DIFFERENT DAY
- ☐ THIS ISN'T FOR ME

CHOOSE YOU CHECK-IN...HOW DID I FEEL?

BEFORE:

- ☐ CALM
- ☐ CHEERFUL
- ☐ IN CONTROL
- ☐ STRESSED
- ☐ DISTRACTED
- ☐ EMOTIONAL
- ☐ OVERWHELMED
- ☐ ANXIOUS
- ☐ ANGRY
- ☐ _____
- ☐ _____

DURING:

- ☐ RELAXED
- ☐ AWESOME
- ☐ STRONG
- ☐ ENERGIZED
- ☐ HAPPY
- ☐ SURPRISED
- ☐ RELIEVED
- ☐ FREE
- ☐ _____
- ☐ _____
- ☐ _____

AFTER:

- ☐ HOPEFUL
- ☐ CONFIDENT
- ☐ PROUD
- ☐ PEACEFUL
- ☐ GROUNDED
- ☐ FOCUSED
- ☐ CONTENT
- ☐ _____
- ☐ _____
- ☐ _____

THIS WAS JUST WHAT I NEEDED BECAUSE...

FEEL-GOOD IDEAS!

Music can change the way you feel. Create a playlist that elevates your mood and listen to it whenever you need a pick-me-up. Use your playlist in the car, at home, or at any moment when you want to bring more joy, energy, and emotional self-care to your day.

MY AWESOME NOTES!

TODAY I CHOSE THIS TYPE OF SELF-CARE:

☐ EMOTIONAL

☐ MENTAL

☐ PHYSICAL

☐ PRACTICAL

☐ SOCIAL

☐ SPIRITUAL

*D*ATE: ....

*T*ODAY'S SELF—CARE
ACTIVITY: ....

....
....
....
....
....
....
....

🍃 TODAY'S 🍃
TAKEAWAY!

☐ MAKE THIS A
REGULAR ACTIVITY

☐ THIS IS GREAT
FOR SPECIAL
OCCASIONS

☐ GIVE THIS ANOTHER
TRY ON A
DIFFERENT DAY

☐ THIS ISN'T FOR ME

*C*HOOSE *Y*OU CHECK-IN...HOW DID I FEEL?

BEFORE:	DURING:	AFTER:
☐ CALM	☐ RELAXED	☐ HOPEFUL
☐ CHEERFUL	☐ AWESOME	☐ CONFIDENT
☐ IN CONTROL	☐ STRONG	☐ PROUD
☐ STRESSED	☐ ENERGIZED	☐ PEACEFUL
☐ DISTRACTED	☐ HAPPY	☐ GROUNDED
☐ EMOTIONAL	☐ SURPRISED	☐ FOCUSED
☐ OVERWHELMED	☐ RELIEVED	☐ CONTENT
☐ ANXIOUS	☐ FREE	☐ _____
☐ ANGRY	☐ _____	☐ _____
☐ _____	☐ _____	☐ _____
☐ _____	☐ _____	

THIS WAS JUST WHAT I NEEDED BECAUSE...

....

....

....

....

....

....

....

....

KEEP IT GOING!

Research has shown it takes at least twenty-one days to form new habits, which means it will take time for self-care to become part of your regular routine. Keep at it and consider planning your self-care activities for the next twenty-one days to help the habits stick.

MY AWESOME NOTES!

....

....

....

....

....

....

....

....

....

....

TODAY I CHOSE THIS TYPE OF SELF-CARE:

☐ EMOTIONAL

☐ MENTAL

☐ PHYSICAL

☐ PRACTICAL

☐ SOCIAL

☐ SPIRITUAL

DATE: ....

TODAY'S SELF-CARE ACTIVITY: ....

....
....
....
....
....
....

TODAY'S TAKEAWAY!

☐ MAKE THIS A REGULAR ACTIVITY

☐ THIS IS GREAT FOR SPECIAL OCCASIONS

☐ GIVE THIS ANOTHER TRY ON A DIFFERENT DAY

☐ THIS ISN'T FOR ME

CHOOSE YOU CHECK-IN...HOW DID I FEEL?

BEFORE:

☐ CALM
☐ CHEERFUL
☐ IN CONTROL
☐ STRESSED
☐ DISTRACTED
☐ EMOTIONAL
☐ OVERWHELMED
☐ ANXIOUS
☐ ANGRY
☐ _____
☐ _____

DURING:

☐ RELAXED
☐ AWESOME
☐ STRONG
☐ ENERGIZED
☐ HAPPY
☐ SURPRISED
☐ RELIEVED
☐ FREE
☐ _____
☐ _____
☐ _____

AFTER:

☐ HOPEFUL
☐ CONFIDENT
☐ PROUD
☐ PEACEFUL
☐ GROUNDED
☐ FOCUSED
☐ CONTENT
☐ _____
☐ _____
☐ _____
☐ _____

THIS WAS JUST WHAT I NEEDED BECAUSE...

....
....
....
....
....
....
....
....

FEEL-GOOD IDEAS!

How much water do you typically drink in a day? Chances are that it's not enough! Staying hydrated is important for your overall well-being and is a critical part of physical self-care. So get a reusable water bottle and refill it as often as needed to reach your water intake goals!

MY AWESOME NOTES!

....
....
....
....
....
....
....
....
....
....
....

TODAY I CHOSE THIS TYPE OF SELF-CARE:

☐ EMOTIONAL

☐ MENTAL

☐ PHYSICAL

☐ PRACTICAL

☐ SOCIAL

☐ SPIRITUAL

DATE: ....

TODAY'S SELF-CARE ACTIVITY: ....

....

....

....

....

....

....

CHOOSE YOU CHECK-IN... HOW DID I FEEL?

BEFORE:	DURING:	AFTER:
☐ CALM	☐ RELAXED	☐ HOPEFUL
☐ CHEERFUL	☐ AWESOME	☐ CONFIDENT
☐ IN CONTROL	☐ STRONG	☐ PROUD
☐ STRESSED	☐ ENERGIZED	☐ PEACEFUL
☐ DISTRACTED	☐ HAPPY	☐ GROUNDED
☐ EMOTIONAL	☐ SURPRISED	☐ FOCUSED
☐ OVERWHELMED	☐ RELIEVED	☐ CONTENT
☐ ANXIOUS	☐ FREE	☐ _____
☐ ANGRY	☐ _____	☐ _____
☐ _____	☐ _____	☐ _____
☐ _____	☐ _____	☐ _____

THIS WAS JUST WHAT I NEEDED BECAUSE...

MY AWESOME NOTES!

TODAY I CHOSE THIS TYPE OF SELF-CARE:

☐ EMOTIONAL

☐ MENTAL

☐ PHYSICAL

☐ PRACTICAL

☐ SOCIAL

☐ SPIRITUAL

Date: ....

Today's self-care
activity: ....

....

....

....

....

....

....

Choose You check-in...how did I feel?

BEFORE:	DURING:	AFTER:
☐ CALM	☐ RELAXED	☐ HOPEFUL
☐ CHEERFUL	☐ AWESOME	☐ CONFIDENT
☐ IN CONTROL	☐ STRONG	☐ PROUD
☐ STRESSED	☐ ENERGIZED	☐ PEACEFUL
☐ DISTRACTED	☐ HAPPY	☐ GROUNDED
☐ EMOTIONAL	☐ SURPRISED	☐ FOCUSED
☐ OVERWHELMED	☐ RELIEVED	☐ CONTENT
☐ ANXIOUS	☐ FREE	☐ _____
☐ ANGRY	☐ _____	☐ _____
☐ _____	☐ _____	☐ _____
☐ _____	☐ _____	☐ _____

THIS WAS JUST WHAT I NEEDED BECAUSE...

....

....

....

....

....

....

....

....

KEEP IT GOING!

Some days you may have "big" self-care activities like a long hike or massage, and other days will be "small" activities like pausing to breathe or listening to a podcast for a few minutes. Self-care of any size is important, so feel good that you did something for yourself!

MY AWESOME NOTES!

....

....

....

....

....

....

....

....

....

....

....

TODAY I CHOSE THIS TYPE OF SELF-CARE:

- ☐ EMOTIONAL
- ☐ MENTAL
- ☐ PHYSICAL
- ☐ PRACTICAL
- ☐ SOCIAL
- ☐ SPIRITUAL

DATE: ....

TODAY'S SELF-CARE ACTIVITY: ....

....

....

....

....

....

- ☐ MAKE THIS A REGULAR ACTIVITY
- ☐ THIS IS GREAT FOR SPECIAL OCCASIONS
- ☐ GIVE THIS ANOTHER TRY ON A DIFFERENT DAY
- ☐ THIS ISN'T FOR ME

CHOOSE YOU CHECK-IN...HOW DID I FEEL?

BEFORE:

- ☐ CALM
- ☐ CHEERFUL
- ☐ IN CONTROL
- ☐ STRESSED
- ☐ DISTRACTED
- ☐ EMOTIONAL
- ☐ OVERWHELMED
- ☐ ANXIOUS
- ☐ ANGRY
- ☐ _____
- ☐ _____

DURING:

- ☐ RELAXED
- ☐ AWESOME
- ☐ STRONG
- ☐ ENERGIZED
- ☐ HAPPY
- ☐ SURPRISED
- ☐ RELIEVED
- ☐ FREE
- ☐ _____
- ☐ _____
- ☐ _____

AFTER:

- ☐ HOPEFUL
- ☐ CONFIDENT
- ☐ PROUD
- ☐ PEACEFUL
- ☐ GROUNDED
- ☐ FOCUSED
- ☐ CONTENT
- ☐ _____
- ☐ _____
- ☐ _____
- ☐ _____

THIS WAS JUST WHAT I NEEDED BECAUSE...

FEEL-GOOD IDEAS! Make a date with someone important: partner, friend, parent, or child. Get that social self-care on the calendar! Bonus points if your date also includes something else that meets your self-care needs, like going for a walk, getting a mani-pedi, or seeing a performer you enjoy.

MY AWESOME NOTES!

TODAY I CHOSE THIS TYPE OF SELF-CARE:

- ☐ EMOTIONAL
- ☐ MENTAL
- ☐ PHYSICAL
- ☐ PRACTICAL
- ☐ SOCIAL
- ☐ SPIRITUAL

DATE: ....

TODAY'S SELF-CARE ACTIVITY: ....

....
....
....
....
....
....

TODAY'S TAKEAWAY!

- ☐ MAKE THIS A REGULAR ACTIVITY
- ☐ THIS IS GREAT FOR SPECIAL OCCASIONS
- ☐ GIVE THIS ANOTHER TRY ON A DIFFERENT DAY
- ☐ THIS ISN'T FOR ME

CHOOSE YOU CHECK-IN...HOW DID I FEEL?

BEFORE:
- ☐ CALM
- ☐ CHEERFUL
- ☐ IN CONTROL
- ☐ STRESSED
- ☐ DISTRACTED
- ☐ EMOTIONAL
- ☐ OVERWHELMED
- ☐ ANXIOUS
- ☐ ANGRY
- ☐ _____
- ☐ _____

DURING:
- ☐ RELAXED
- ☐ AWESOME
- ☐ STRONG
- ☐ ENERGIZED
- ☐ HAPPY
- ☐ SURPRISED
- ☐ RELIEVED
- ☐ FREE
- ☐ _____
- ☐ _____
- ☐ _____

AFTER:
- ☐ HOPEFUL
- ☐ CONFIDENT
- ☐ PROUD
- ☐ PEACEFUL
- ☐ GROUNDED
- ☐ FOCUSED
- ☐ CONTENT
- ☐ _____
- ☐ _____
- ☐ _____

THIS WAS JUST WHAT I NEEDED BECAUSE...

....

....

....

....

....

....

....

....

KEEP IT GOING!
When life gets busy, self-care is usually the first thing that falls by the wayside. Instead, try to add in more self-care, but focus on activities that can be done quickly and that help relieve stress. Keep a list of five to ten quick activities you can add in whenever you need them!

MY AWESOME NOTES!

....

....

....

....

....

....

....

....

....

....

....

TODAY I CHOSE THIS TYPE OF SELF-CARE:

☐ EMOTIONAL

☐ MENTAL

☐ PHYSICAL

☐ PRACTICAL

☐ SOCIAL

☐ SPIRITUAL

DATE:
TODAY'S SELF-CARE ACTIVITY:

- ☐ MAKE THIS A REGULAR ACTIVITY
- ☐ THIS IS GREAT FOR SPECIAL OCCASIONS
- ☐ GIVE THIS ANOTHER TRY ON A DIFFERENT DAY
- ☐ THIS ISN'T FOR ME

CHOOSE YOU CHECK-IN...HOW DID I FEEL?

BEFORE:
- ☐ CALM
- ☐ CHEERFUL
- ☐ IN CONTROL
- ☐ STRESSED
- ☐ DISTRACTED
- ☐ EMOTIONAL
- ☐ OVERWHELMED
- ☐ ANXIOUS
- ☐ ANGRY
- ☐ _____
- ☐ _____

DURING:
- ☐ RELAXED
- ☐ AWESOME
- ☐ STRONG
- ☐ ENERGIZED
- ☐ HAPPY
- ☐ SURPRISED
- ☐ RELIEVED
- ☐ FREE
- ☐ _____
- ☐ _____

AFTER:
- ☐ HOPEFUL
- ☐ CONFIDENT
- ☐ PROUD
- ☐ PEACEFUL
- ☐ GROUNDED
- ☐ FOCUSED
- ☐ CONTENT
- ☐ _____
- ☐ _____
- ☐ _____

THIS WAS JUST WHAT I NEEDED BECAUSE...

FEEL-GOOD IDEAS!

Declutter something! Pick one area of your house and keep only what's essential. Recycle what you can, put giveaways in a bag, and toss anything that's broken. Enjoy the practical self-care that leads to this simplified, less cluttered space—and the positive emotions that come with it!

MY AWESOME NOTES!

TODAY I CHOSE THIS TYPE OF SELF-CARE:

- ☐ EMOTIONAL
- ☐ MENTAL
- ☐ PHYSICAL
- ☐ PRACTICAL
- ☐ SOCIAL
- ☐ SPIRITUAL

Date: ....

Today's self-care activity: ....

....

....

....

....

....

....

TODAY'S — TAKEAWAY!

☐ MAKE THIS A REGULAR ACTIVITY

☐ THIS IS GREAT FOR SPECIAL OCCASIONS

☐ GIVE THIS ANOTHER TRY ON A DIFFERENT DAY

☐ THIS ISN'T FOR ME

Choose You check-in...HOW DID I FEEL?

BEFORE:	DURING:	AFTER:
☐ CALM	☐ RELAXED	☐ HOPEFUL
☐ CHEERFUL	☐ AWESOME	☐ CONFIDENT
☐ IN CONTROL	☐ STRONG	☐ PROUD
☐ STRESSED	☐ ENERGIZED	☐ PEACEFUL
☐ DISTRACTED	☐ HAPPY	☐ GROUNDED
☐ EMOTIONAL	☐ SURPRISED	☐ FOCUSED
☐ OVERWHELMED	☐ RELIEVED	☐ CONTENT
☐ ANXIOUS	☐ FREE	☐ _____
☐ ANGRY	☐ _____	☐ _____
☐ _____	☐ _____	☐ _____
☐ _____	☐ _____	☐ _____

THIS WAS JUST WHAT I NEEDED BECAUSE...

MY AWESOME NOTES!

TODAY I CHOSE THIS TYPE OF SELF–CARE:

☐ EMOTIONAL

☐ MENTAL

☐ PHYSICAL

☐ PRACTICAL

☐ SOCIAL

☐ SPIRITUAL

Date: ....

Today's self-care activity:

....
....
....
....
....
....

- ☐ MAKE THIS A REGULAR ACTIVITY
- ☐ THIS IS GREAT FOR SPECIAL OCCASIONS
- ☐ GIVE THIS ANOTHER TRY ON A DIFFERENT DAY
- ☐ THIS ISN'T FOR ME

Choose You check-in...HOW DID I FEEL?

BEFORE:	DURING:	AFTER:
☐ CALM	☐ RELAXED	☐ HOPEFUL
☐ CHEERFUL	☐ AWESOME	☐ CONFIDENT
☐ IN CONTROL	☐ STRONG	☐ PROUD
☐ STRESSED	☐ ENERGIZED	☐ PEACEFUL
☐ DISTRACTED	☐ HAPPY	☐ GROUNDED
☐ EMOTIONAL	☐ SURPRISED	☐ FOCUSED
☐ OVERWHELMED	☐ RELIEVED	☐ CONTENT
☐ ANXIOUS	☐ FREE	☐ _____
☐ ANGRY	☐ _____	☐ _____
☐ _____	☐ _____	☐ _____
☐ _____	☐ _____	☐ _____

THIS WAS JUST WHAT I NEEDED BECAUSE...

MY AWESOME NOTES!

TODAY I CHOSE THIS TYPE OF SELF-CARE:

☐ EMOTIONAL

☐ MENTAL

☐ PHYSICAL

☐ PRACTICAL

☐ SOCIAL

☐ SPIRITUAL

DATE: ....

TODAY'S SELF—CARE ACTIVITY: ....

....
....
....
....
....
....

TODAY'S TAKEAWAY!

☐ MAKE THIS A REGULAR ACTIVITY

☐ THIS IS GREAT FOR SPECIAL OCCASIONS

☐ GIVE THIS ANOTHER TRY ON A DIFFERENT DAY

☐ THIS ISN'T FOR ME

CHOOSE YOU CHECK-IN...HOW DID I FEEL?

BEFORE:

☐ CALM
☐ CHEERFUL
☐ IN CONTROL
☐ STRESSED
☐ DISTRACTED
☐ EMOTIONAL
☐ OVERWHELMED
☐ ANXIOUS
☐ ANGRY
☐ _____
☐ _____

DURING:

☐ RELAXED
☐ AWESOME
☐ STRONG
☐ ENERGIZED
☐ HAPPY
☐ SURPRISED
☐ RELIEVED
☐ FREE
☐ _____
☐ _____
☐ _____

AFTER:

☐ HOPEFUL
☐ CONFIDENT
☐ PROUD
☐ PEACEFUL
☐ GROUNDED
☐ FOCUSED
☐ CONTENT
☐ _____
☐ _____
☐ _____

THIS WAS JUST WHAT I NEEDED BECAUSE...

....
....
....
....
....
....
....
....

KEEP IT GOING!
Though it can be uncomfortable, saying no sometimes is critical for self-care. When you say no to one thing, you're able to say yes to something else, such as time for yourself or an activity or event that is more fulfilling than what you originally declined.

MY AWESOME NOTES!

....
....
....
....
....
....
....
....
....
....
....
....

TODAY I CHOSE THIS TYPE OF SELF-CARE:

☐ EMOTIONAL

☐ MENTAL

☐ PHYSICAL

☐ PRACTICAL

☐ SOCIAL

☐ SPIRITUAL

DATE:

TODAY'S SELF-CARE ACTIVITY:

TODAY'S TAKEAWAY!

- ☐ MAKE THIS A REGULAR ACTIVITY
- ☐ THIS IS GREAT FOR SPECIAL OCCASIONS
- ☐ GIVE THIS ANOTHER TRY ON A DIFFERENT DAY
- ☐ THIS ISN'T FOR ME

CHOOSE YOU CHECK-IN...HOW DID I FEEL?

BEFORE:	DURING:	AFTER:
☐ CALM	☐ RELAXED	☐ HOPEFUL
☐ CHEERFUL	☐ AWESOME	☐ CONFIDENT
☐ IN CONTROL	☐ STRONG	☐ PROUD
☐ STRESSED	☐ ENERGIZED	☐ PEACEFUL
☐ DISTRACTED	☐ HAPPY	☐ GROUNDED
☐ EMOTIONAL	☐ SURPRISED	☐ FOCUSED
☐ OVERWHELMED	☐ RELIEVED	☐ CONTENT
☐ ANXIOUS	☐ FREE	☐ _____
☐ ANGRY	☐ _____	☐ _____
☐ _____	☐ _____	☐ _____
☐ _____	☐ _____	☐ _____

This was just what I needed because...

....

....

....

....

....

....

....

....

FEEL-GOOD IDEAS!

Essential oils like lavender and frankincense can help you relax and de-stress, which improves your mental and emotional state. You can add a few drops to a diffuser, rub a drop on your hands and inhale deeply, or massage a drop onto your pulse points or the bottoms of your feet.

My awesome notes!

....

....

....

....

....

....

....

....

....

Today I chose this type of self-care:

☐ EMOTIONAL

☐ MENTAL

☐ PHYSICAL

☐ PRACTICAL

☐ SOCIAL

☐ SPIRITUAL

DATE: ....

TODAY'S SELF-CARE ACTIVITY: ....

....

....

....

....

....

....

TODAY'S —— ——TAKEAWAY!

☐ MAKE THIS A REGULAR ACTIVITY

☐ THIS IS GREAT FOR SPECIAL OCCASIONS

☐ GIVE THIS ANOTHER TRY ON A DIFFERENT DAY

☐ THIS ISN'T FOR ME

CHOOSE YOU CHECK-IN... HOW DID I FEEL?

BEFORE:

☐ CALM
☐ CHEERFUL
☐ IN CONTROL
☐ STRESSED
☐ DISTRACTED
☐ EMOTIONAL
☐ OVERWHELMED
☐ ANXIOUS
☐ ANGRY
☐ _____
☐ _____

DURING:

☐ RELAXED
☐ AWESOME
☐ STRONG
☐ ENERGIZED
☐ HAPPY
☐ SURPRISED
☐ RELIEVED
☐ FREE
☐ _____
☐ _____
☐ _____

AFTER:

☐ HOPEFUL
☐ CONFIDENT
☐ PROUD
☐ PEACEFUL
☐ GROUNDED
☐ FOCUSED
☐ CONTENT
☐ _____
☐ _____
☐ _____

THIS WAS JUST WHAT I NEEDED BECAUSE...

STAY INSPIRED!

"Women in particular need to keep an eye on their physical and mental health, because if we're scurrying to and from appointments and errands, we don't have a lot of time to take care of ourselves. We need to do a better job of putting ourselves higher on our own 'to-do' list."

—Michelle Obama, former US first lady

MY AWESOME NOTES!

TODAY I CHOSE THIS TYPE OF SELF-CARE:

☐ EMOTIONAL

☐ MENTAL

☐ PHYSICAL

☐ PRACTICAL

☐ SOCIAL

☐ SPIRITUAL

Date: ....

Today's self-care activity: ....

....

....

....

....

....

Choose You check-in...HOW DID I FEEL?

BEFORE:	*DURING:*	*AFTER:*
☐ CALM	☐ RELAXED	☐ HOPEFUL
☐ CHEERFUL	☐ AWESOME	☐ CONFIDENT
☐ IN CONTROL	☐ STRONG	☐ PROUD
☐ STRESSED	☐ ENERGIZED	☐ PEACEFUL
☐ DISTRACTED	☐ HAPPY	☐ GROUNDED
☐ EMOTIONAL	☐ SURPRISED	☐ FOCUSED
☐ OVERWHELMED	☐ RELIEVED	☐ CONTENT
☐ ANXIOUS	☐ FREE	☐ _____
☐ ANGRY	☐ _____	☐ _____
☐ _____	☐ _____	☐ _____
☐ _____	☐ _____	☐ _____

THIS WAS JUST WHAT I NEEDED BECAUSE...

KEEP IT GOING!

There are fantastic ways to utilize technology for self-care, such as downloading meditation apps to your phone or streaming workouts to do at home. However, you can also easily waste time that's critical for self-care, so monitor your tech use and make sure the time you spend online is purposeful and meaningful.

MY AWESOME NOTES!

TODAY I CHOSE THIS TYPE OF SELF-CARE:

☐ EMOTIONAL

☐ MENTAL

☐ PHYSICAL

☐ PRACTICAL

☐ SOCIAL

☐ SPIRITUAL

DATE: ....

TODAY'S SELF-CARE ACTIVITY: ....

....

....

....

....

....

....

....

TODAY'S —— —— TAKEAWAY!

☐ MAKE THIS A REGULAR ACTIVITY

☐ THIS IS GREAT FOR SPECIAL OCCASIONS

☐ GIVE THIS ANOTHER TRY ON A DIFFERENT DAY

☐ THIS ISN'T FOR ME

CHOOSE YOU CHECK-IN... HOW DID I FEEL?

BEFORE:	DURING:	AFTER:
☐ CALM	☐ RELAXED	☐ HOPEFUL
☐ CHEERFUL	☐ AWESOME	☐ CONFIDENT
☐ IN CONTROL	☐ STRONG	☐ PROUD
☐ STRESSED	☐ ENERGIZED	☐ PEACEFUL
☐ DISTRACTED	☐ HAPPY	☐ GROUNDED
☐ EMOTIONAL	☐ SURPRISED	☐ FOCUSED
☐ OVERWHELMED	☐ RELIEVED	☐ CONTENT
☐ ANXIOUS	☐ FREE	☐ _____
☐ ANGRY	☐ _____	☐ _____
☐ _____	☐ _____	☐ _____
☐ _____	☐ _____	☐ _____

THIS WAS JUST WHAT I NEEDED BECAUSE...

MY AWESOME NOTES!

TODAY I CHOSE THIS TYPE OF SELF-CARE:

- ☐ EMOTIONAL
- ☐ MENTAL
- ☐ PHYSICAL
- ☐ PRACTICAL
- ☐ SOCIAL
- ☐ SPIRITUAL

DATE: ....

TODAY'S SELF-CARE ACTIVITY: ....

....

....

....

....

....

....

CHOOSE YOU CHECK-IN...HOW DID I FEEL?

BEFORE:	DURING:	AFTER:
☐ CALM	☐ RELAXED	☐ HOPEFUL
☐ CHEERFUL	☐ AWESOME	☐ CONFIDENT
☐ IN CONTROL	☐ STRONG	☐ PROUD
☐ STRESSED	☐ ENERGIZED	☐ PEACEFUL
☐ DISTRACTED	☐ HAPPY	☐ GROUNDED
☐ EMOTIONAL	☐ SURPRISED	☐ FOCUSED
☐ OVERWHELMED	☐ RELIEVED	☐ CONTENT
☐ ANXIOUS	☐ FREE	☐ _____
☐ ANGRY	☐ _____	☐ _____
☐ _____	☐ _____	☐ _____
☐ _____	☐ _____	☐ _____

THIS WAS JUST WHAT I NEEDED BECAUSE...

....

....

....

....

....

....

....

....

....

KEEP IT GOING!

Remember that self-care isn't just baths and beauty treatments: self-care gets to the core of what you need to be your best. Sometimes this "work" is fun and relaxing, but other times you need to tackle the hard stuff. The hard stuff is also self-care, and you need to make time for it to ensure you meet all your different needs.

MY AWESOME NOTES!

....

....

....

....

....

....

....

....

....

....

TODAY I CHOSE THIS TYPE OF SELF-CARE:

☐ EMOTIONAL

☐ MENTAL

☐ PHYSICAL

☐ PRACTICAL

☐ SOCIAL

☐ SPIRITUAL

Date: ....

*Today's self-care
activity:* ....

....
....
....
....
....
....

☐ MAKE THIS A
REGULAR ACTIVITY

☐ THIS IS GREAT
FOR SPECIAL
OCCASIONS

☐ GIVE THIS ANOTHER
TRY ON A
DIFFERENT DAY

☐ THIS ISN'T FOR ME

CHOOSE YOU CHECK-IN...HOW DID I FEEL?

BEFORE:	DURING:	AFTER:
☐ CALM	☐ RELAXED	☐ HOPEFUL
☐ CHEERFUL	☐ AWESOME	☐ CONFIDENT
☐ IN CONTROL	☐ STRONG	☐ PROUD
☐ STRESSED	☐ ENERGIZED	☐ PEACEFUL
☐ DISTRACTED	☐ HAPPY	☐ GROUNDED
☐ EMOTIONAL	☐ SURPRISED	☐ FOCUSED
☐ OVERWHELMED	☐ RELIEVED	☐ CONTENT
☐ ANXIOUS	☐ FREE	☐ _____
☐ ANGRY	☐ _____	☐ _____
☐ _____	☐ _____	☐ _____
☐ _____	☐ _____	☐ _____

THIS WAS JUST WHAT I NEEDED BECAUSE...

FEEL-GOOD IDEAS!

Starting the day well-rested fulfills your physical, emotional, and mental needs. So if you find yourself staying up too late, set a goal for your bedtime and begin winding down earlier than usual. Set a gentle alarm if needed to remind you to start shifting into sleep mode.

MY AWESOME NOTES!

TODAY I CHOSE THIS TYPE OF SELF-CARE:

- ☐ EMOTIONAL
- ☐ MENTAL
- ☐ PHYSICAL
- ☐ PRACTICAL
- ☐ SOCIAL
- ☐ SPIRITUAL

DATE: ....

TODAY'S SELF-CARE ACTIVITY: ....

....

....

....

....

....

....

....

CHOOSE YOU CHECK-IN...HOW DID I FEEL?

BEFORE:	*DURING:*	*AFTER:*
☐ CALM	☐ RELAXED	☐ HOPEFUL
☐ CHEERFUL	☐ AWESOME	☐ CONFIDENT
☐ IN CONTROL	☐ STRONG	☐ PROUD
☐ STRESSED	☐ ENERGIZED	☐ PEACEFUL
☐ DISTRACTED	☐ HAPPY	☐ GROUNDED
☐ EMOTIONAL	☐ SURPRISED	☐ FOCUSED
☐ OVERWHELMED	☐ RELIEVED	☐ CONTENT
☐ ANXIOUS	☐ FREE	☐ _____
☐ ANGRY	☐ _____	☐ _____
☐ _____	☐ _____	☐ _____
☐ _____	☐ _____	

THIS WAS JUST WHAT I NEEDED BECAUSE...

....
....
....
....
....
....
....

KEEP IT GOING!

Sometimes it's easier to prioritize self-care when it involves someone else. This can help you stay accountable and meet your social self-care needs. And it can make self-care even more fun!

MY AWESOME NOTES!

....
....
....
....
....
....
....
....
....
....
....
....

TODAY I CHOSE THIS TYPE OF SELF-CARE:

☐ EMOTIONAL

☐ MENTAL

☐ PHYSICAL

☐ PRACTICAL

☐ SOCIAL

☐ SPIRITUAL

*D*ATE: ....

*T*ODAY'S SELF–CARE
ACTIVITY: ....

....

....

....

....

....

....

TODAY'S TAKEAWAY!

☐ MAKE THIS A REGULAR ACTIVITY

☐ THIS IS GREAT FOR SPECIAL OCCASIONS

☐ GIVE THIS ANOTHER TRY ON A DIFFERENT DAY

☐ THIS ISN'T FOR ME

*C*HOOSE *Y*OU CHECK–IN...HOW DID I FEEL?

BEFORE:	*DURING:*	*AFTER:*
☐ CALM	☐ RELAXED	☐ HOPEFUL
☐ CHEERFUL	☐ AWESOME	☐ CONFIDENT
☐ IN CONTROL	☐ STRONG	☐ PROUD
☐ STRESSED	☐ ENERGIZED	☐ PEACEFUL
☐ DISTRACTED	☐ HAPPY	☐ GROUNDED
☐ EMOTIONAL	☐ SURPRISED	☐ FOCUSED
☐ OVERWHELMED	☐ RELIEVED	☐ CONTENT
☐ ANXIOUS	☐ FREE	☐ _____
☐ ANGRY	☐ _____	☐ _____
☐ _____	☐ _____	☐ _____
☐ _____	☐ _____	☐ _____

THIS WAS JUST WHAT I NEEDED BECAUSE...

FEEL-GOOD IDEAS!

Prioritize mental self-care with a "mental-health day" (or a "mental-health hour" if that's what you have time for). Fill that time with anything that makes you feel good: mindless TV, delicious food, praying, writing, sleeping, sitting outside—the options are endless!

MY AWESOME NOTES!

TODAY I CHOSE THIS TYPE OF SELF-CARE:

- ☐ EMOTIONAL
- ☐ MENTAL
- ☐ PHYSICAL
- ☐ PRACTICAL
- ☐ SOCIAL
- ☐ SPIRITUAL

Date: ....

Today's self-care
activity: ....

....
....
....
....
....
....
....

Choose You check-in... HOW DID I FEEL?

BEFORE:	DURING:	AFTER:
☐ CALM	☐ RELAXED	☐ HOPEFUL
☐ CHEERFUL	☐ AWESOME	☐ CONFIDENT
☐ IN CONTROL	☐ STRONG	☐ PROUD
☐ STRESSED	☐ ENERGIZED	☐ PEACEFUL
☐ DISTRACTED	☐ HAPPY	☐ GROUNDED
☐ EMOTIONAL	☐ SURPRISED	☐ FOCUSED
☐ OVERWHELMED	☐ RELIEVED	☐ CONTENT
☐ ANXIOUS	☐ FREE	☐ _____
☐ ANGRY	☐ _____	☐ _____
☐ _____	☐ _____	☐ _____
☐ _____	☐ _____	☐ _____

THIS WAS JUST WHAT I NEEDED BECAUSE...

MY AWESOME NOTES!

TODAY I CHOSE THIS TYPE OF SELF-CARE:

☐ EMOTIONAL

☐ MENTAL

☐ PHYSICAL

☐ PRACTICAL

☐ SOCIAL

☐ SPIRITUAL

DATE:

TODAY'S SELF-CARE ACTIVITY:

TODAY'S TAKEAWAY!

☐ MAKE THIS A REGULAR ACTIVITY

☐ THIS IS GREAT FOR SPECIAL OCCASIONS

☐ GIVE THIS ANOTHER TRY ON A DIFFERENT DAY

☐ THIS ISN'T FOR ME

CHOOSE YOU CHECK-IN...HOW DID I FEEL?

BEFORE:	DURING:	AFTER:
☐ CALM	☐ RELAXED	☐ HOPEFUL
☐ CHEERFUL	☐ AWESOME	☐ CONFIDENT
☐ IN CONTROL	☐ STRONG	☐ PROUD
☐ STRESSED	☐ ENERGIZED	☐ PEACEFUL
☐ DISTRACTED	☐ HAPPY	☐ GROUNDED
☐ EMOTIONAL	☐ SURPRISED	☐ FOCUSED
☐ OVERWHELMED	☐ RELIEVED	☐ CONTENT
☐ ANXIOUS	☐ FREE	☐ _____
☐ ANGRY	☐ _____	☐ _____
☐ _____	☐ _____	☐ _____
☐ _____	☐ _____	☐ _____

THIS WAS JUST WHAT I NEEDED BECAUSE...

....
....
....
....
....
....
....
....

KEEP IT GOING!

If you're looking to increase your physical self-care, start where you are and do what works for you. You can start with a simple five-minute walk a few times a week and build from there once you have a consistent routine. We all start somewhere, and something is better than nothing!

MY AWESOME NOTES!

....
....
....
....
....
....
....
....
....
....
....
....

TODAY I CHOSE THIS TYPE OF SELF-CARE:

☐ EMOTIONAL

☐ MENTAL

☐ PHYSICAL

☐ PRACTICAL

☐ SOCIAL

☐ SPIRITUAL

DATE: ....

TODAY'S SELF-CARE ACTIVITY: ....

....
....
....
....
....
....
....

- ☐ **MAKE THIS A REGULAR ACTIVITY**
- ☐ **THIS IS GREAT FOR SPECIAL OCCASIONS**
- ☐ **GIVE THIS ANOTHER TRY ON A DIFFERENT DAY**
- ☐ **THIS ISN'T FOR ME**

CHOOSE YOU CHECK-IN...HOW DID I FEEL?

BEFORE:	DURING:	AFTER:
☐ CALM	☐ RELAXED	☐ HOPEFUL
☐ CHEERFUL	☐ AWESOME	☐ CONFIDENT
☐ IN CONTROL	☐ STRONG	☐ PROUD
☐ STRESSED	☐ ENERGIZED	☐ PEACEFUL
☐ DISTRACTED	☐ HAPPY	☐ GROUNDED
☐ EMOTIONAL	☐ SURPRISED	☐ FOCUSED
☐ OVERWHELMED	☐ RELIEVED	☐ CONTENT
☐ ANXIOUS	☐ FREE	☐ _____
☐ ANGRY	☐ _____	☐ _____
☐ _____	☐ _____	☐ _____
☐ _____	☐ _____	☐ _____

THIS WAS JUST WHAT I NEEDED BECAUSE...

....
....
....
....
....
....
....
....
....

FEEL-GOOD IDEAS! Do a self-care product swap with friends! Meet up at someone's house with snacks and drinks and have everyone bring their favorite self-care item like a candle, diffuser, book, or face mask. Then have everyone swap! Not only do you get social self-care, but everyone takes home something new.

MY AWESOME NOTES!

....
....
....
....
....
....
....
....
....
....

TODAY I CHOSE THIS TYPE OF SELF-CARE:

☐ EMOTIONAL

☐ MENTAL

☐ PHYSICAL

☐ PRACTICAL

☐ SOCIAL

☐ SPIRITUAL

DATE:

TODAY'S SELF-CARE ACTIVITY:

CHOOSE YOU CHECK-IN...HOW DID I FEEL?

BEFORE:	DURING:	AFTER:
☐ CALM	☐ RELAXED	☐ HOPEFUL
☐ CHEERFUL	☐ AWESOME	☐ CONFIDENT
☐ IN CONTROL	☐ STRONG	☐ PROUD
☐ STRESSED	☐ ENERGIZED	☐ PEACEFUL
☐ DISTRACTED	☐ HAPPY	☐ GROUNDED
☐ EMOTIONAL	☐ SURPRISED	☐ FOCUSED
☐ OVERWHELMED	☐ RELIEVED	☐ CONTENT
☐ ANXIOUS	☐ FREE	☐ _____
☐ ANGRY	☐ _____	☐ _____
☐ _____	☐ _____	☐ _____
☐ _____	☐ _____	☐ _____

THIS WAS JUST WHAT I NEEDED BECAUSE...

....

....

....

....

....

....

....

....

....

KEEP IT GOING!

Self-care is such a positive choice, but making it happen can sometimes feel difficult. Continue to focus on the benefits of daily self-care in those moments when you need an extra push to choose you!

MY AWESOME NOTES!

....

....

....

....

....

....

....

....

....

....

....

....

TODAY I CHOSE THIS TYPE OF SELF-CARE:

☐ EMOTIONAL

☐ MENTAL

☐ PHYSICAL

☐ PRACTICAL

☐ SOCIAL

☐ SPIRITUAL

DATE: ....

TODAY'S SELF-CARE ACTIVITY: ....

....

....

....

....

....

....

TODAY'S TAKEAWAY!

- ☐ MAKE THIS A REGULAR ACTIVITY
- ☐ THIS IS GREAT FOR SPECIAL OCCASIONS
- ☐ GIVE THIS ANOTHER TRY ON A DIFFERENT DAY
- ☐ THIS ISN'T FOR ME

CHOOSE YOU CHECK-IN...HOW DID I FEEL?

BEFORE:

- ☐ CALM
- ☐ CHEERFUL
- ☐ IN CONTROL
- ☐ STRESSED
- ☐ DISTRACTED
- ☐ EMOTIONAL
- ☐ OVERWHELMED
- ☐ ANXIOUS
- ☐ ANGRY
- ☐ _____
- ☐ _____

DURING:

- ☐ RELAXED
- ☐ AWESOME
- ☐ STRONG
- ☐ ENERGIZED
- ☐ HAPPY
- ☐ SURPRISED
- ☐ RELIEVED
- ☐ FREE
- ☐ _____
- ☐ _____

AFTER:

- ☐ HOPEFUL
- ☐ CONFIDENT
- ☐ PROUD
- ☐ PEACEFUL
- ☐ GROUNDED
- ☐ FOCUSED
- ☐ CONTENT
- ☐ _____
- ☐ _____
- ☐ _____

THIS WAS JUST WHAT I NEEDED BECAUSE...

....

....

....

....

....

....

....

....

FEEL-GOOD IDEAS!

Pray. No matter your religion, or lack thereof, take the time to pray. Through spiritual self-care, you can create a greater sense of peace and a stronger connection to yourself, as well as a connection with any higher power you believe in.

MY AWESOME NOTES!

....

....

....

....

....

....

....

....

....

....

....

TODAY I CHOSE THIS TYPE OF SELF-CARE:

☐ EMOTIONAL

☐ MENTAL

☐ PHYSICAL

☐ PRACTICAL

☐ SOCIAL

☐ SPIRITUAL

DATE: ....

TODAY'S SELF-CARE ACTIVITY: ....

....

....

....

....

....

....

- ☐ MAKE THIS A REGULAR ACTIVITY
- ☐ THIS IS GREAT FOR SPECIAL OCCASIONS
- ☐ GIVE THIS ANOTHER TRY ON A DIFFERENT DAY
- ☐ THIS ISN'T FOR ME

CHOOSE YOU CHECK-IN...HOW DID I FEEL?

BEFORE:

- ☐ CALM
- ☐ CHEERFUL
- ☐ IN CONTROL
- ☐ STRESSED
- ☐ DISTRACTED
- ☐ EMOTIONAL
- ☐ OVERWHELMED
- ☐ ANXIOUS
- ☐ ANGRY
- ☐ _____
- ☐ _____

DURING:

- ☐ RELAXED
- ☐ AWESOME
- ☐ STRONG
- ☐ ENERGIZED
- ☐ HAPPY
- ☐ SURPRISED
- ☐ RELIEVED
- ☐ FREE
- ☐ _____
- ☐ _____

AFTER:

- ☐ HOPEFUL
- ☐ CONFIDENT
- ☐ PROUD
- ☐ PEACEFUL
- ☐ GROUNDED
- ☐ FOCUSED
- ☐ CONTENT
- ☐ _____
- ☐ _____
- ☐ _____

THIS WAS JUST WHAT I NEEDED BECAUSE...

MY AWESOME NOTES!

TODAY I CHOSE THIS TYPE OF SELF-CARE:

☐ EMOTIONAL

☐ MENTAL

☐ PHYSICAL

☐ PRACTICAL

☐ SOCIAL

☐ SPIRITUAL

DATE: ....

TODAY'S SELF-CARE
ACTIVITY: ....

....
....
....
....
....
....

☐ MAKE THIS A REGULAR ACTIVITY

☐ THIS IS GREAT FOR SPECIAL OCCASIONS

☐ GIVE THIS ANOTHER TRY ON A DIFFERENT DAY

☐ THIS ISN'T FOR ME

CHOOSE YOU CHECK-IN...HOW DID I FEEL?

BEFORE:	DURING:	AFTER:
☐ CALM	☐ RELAXED	☐ HOPEFUL
☐ CHEERFUL	☐ AWESOME	☐ CONFIDENT
☐ IN CONTROL	☐ STRONG	☐ PROUD
☐ STRESSED	☐ ENERGIZED	☐ PEACEFUL
☐ DISTRACTED	☐ HAPPY	☐ GROUNDED
☐ EMOTIONAL	☐ SURPRISED	☐ FOCUSED
☐ OVERWHELMED	☐ RELIEVED	☐ CONTENT
☐ ANXIOUS	☐ FREE	☐ _____
☐ ANGRY	☐ _____	☐ _____
☐ _____	☐ _____	☐ _____
☐ _____	☐ _____	☐ _____

THIS WAS JUST WHAT I NEEDED BECAUSE...

FEEL-GOOD IDEAS!

Use technology to meet all your self-care needs. You can find lots of free and inexpensive apps for all types of self-care, including meditation, mindfulness activities, and decluttering checklists. You can even find apps that make communication (and improving your social self-care needs) easier.

MY AWESOME NOTES!

TODAY I CHOSE THIS TYPE OF SELF-CARE:

☐ EMOTIONAL

☐ MENTAL

☐ PHYSICAL

☐ PRACTICAL

☐ SOCIAL

☐ SPIRITUAL

DATE: ....

TODAY'S SELF—CARE ACTIVITY: ....

....
....
....
....
....
....

🍃 TODAY'S 🍃 TAKEAWAY!

- ☐ MAKE THIS A REGULAR ACTIVITY
- ☐ THIS IS GREAT FOR SPECIAL OCCASIONS
- ☐ GIVE THIS ANOTHER TRY ON A DIFFERENT DAY
- ☐ THIS ISN'T FOR ME

CHOOSE YOU CHECK-IN...HOW DID I FEEL?

BEFORE:	DURING:	AFTER:
☐ CALM	☐ RELAXED	☐ HOPEFUL
☐ CHEERFUL	☐ AWESOME	☐ CONFIDENT
☐ IN CONTROL	☐ STRONG	☐ PROUD
☐ STRESSED	☐ ENERGIZED	☐ PEACEFUL
☐ DISTRACTED	☐ HAPPY	☐ GROUNDED
☐ EMOTIONAL	☐ SURPRISED	☐ FOCUSED
☐ OVERWHELMED	☐ RELIEVED	☐ CONTENT
☐ ANXIOUS	☐ FREE	☐ _____
☐ ANGRY	☐ _____	☐ _____
☐ _____	☐ _____	☐ _____
☐ _____		

THIS WAS JUST WHAT I NEEDED BECAUSE...

....

....

....

....

....

....

....

....

KEEP IT GOING!
Simplify your
self-care to get it
done! Do whatever you need to
do to make it as easy as possible
to complete your self-care activities.
For example, always keep your yoga mat
in the same place, set a monthly
appointment for a massage, or use
a subscription box that's
delivered regularly.

MY AWESOME NOTES!

....

....

....

....

....

....

....

....

....

....

....

TODAY I CHOSE THIS TYPE OF SELF-CARE:

☐ EMOTIONAL

☐ MENTAL

☐ PHYSICAL

☐ PRACTICAL

☐ SOCIAL

☐ SPIRITUAL

DATE: ....

TODAY'S SELF-CARE ACTIVITY: ....

....

....

....

....

....

☐ MAKE THIS A REGULAR ACTIVITY

☐ THIS IS GREAT FOR SPECIAL OCCASIONS

☐ GIVE THIS ANOTHER TRY ON A DIFFERENT DAY

☐ THIS ISN'T FOR ME

CHOOSE YOU CHECK-IN...HOW DID I FEEL?

BEFORE:	DURING:	AFTER:
☐ CALM	☐ RELAXED	☐ HOPEFUL
☐ CHEERFUL	☐ AWESOME	☐ CONFIDENT
☐ IN CONTROL	☐ STRONG	☐ PROUD
☐ STRESSED	☐ ENERGIZED	☐ PEACEFUL
☐ DISTRACTED	☐ HAPPY	☐ GROUNDED
☐ EMOTIONAL	☐ SURPRISED	☐ FOCUSED
☐ OVERWHELMED	☐ RELIEVED	☐ CONTENT
☐ ANXIOUS	☐ FREE	☐ _____
☐ ANGRY	☐ _____	☐ _____
☐ _____	☐ _____	☐ _____
☐ _____	☐ _____	☐ _____

THIS WAS JUST WHAT I NEEDED BECAUSE...

....
....
....
....
....
....
....

FEEL-GOOD IDEAS!

For mental self-care, create affirmations: positive statements that give you something to focus on, help to block out negative thinking, and build your confidence. Examples include "I am amazing," "I am enough," and "I can handle this." Repeat your affirmations over and over, using them as often as you need.

MY AWESOME NOTES!

....
....
....
....
....
....
....
....
....
....

TODAY I CHOSE THIS TYPE OF SELF-CARE:

☐ EMOTIONAL

☐ MENTAL

☐ PHYSICAL

☐ PRACTICAL

☐ SOCIAL

☐ SPIRITUAL

DATE: ....

TODAY'S SELF-CARE ACTIVITY: ....

....
....
....
....
....
....
....

Choose You check-in... HOW DID I FEEL?

BEFORE:

☐ CALM
☐ CHEERFUL
☐ IN CONTROL
☐ STRESSED
☐ DISTRACTED
☐ EMOTIONAL
☐ OVERWHELMED
☐ ANXIOUS
☐ ANGRY
☐ _____
☐ _____

DURING:

☐ RELAXED
☐ AWESOME
☐ STRONG
☐ ENERGIZED
☐ HAPPY
☐ SURPRISED
☐ RELIEVED
☐ FREE
☐ _____
☐ _____
☐ _____

AFTER:

☐ HOPEFUL
☐ CONFIDENT
☐ PROUD
☐ PEACEFUL
☐ GROUNDED
☐ FOCUSED
☐ CONTENT
☐ _____
☐ _____
☐ _____

THIS WAS JUST WHAT I NEEDED BECAUSE...

....

....

....

....

....

....

....

....

MY AWESOME NOTES!

....

....

....

....

....

....

....

....

....

....

....

TODAY I CHOSE THIS TYPE OF SELF-CARE:

☐ EMOTIONAL

☐ MENTAL

☐ PHYSICAL

☐ PRACTICAL

☐ SOCIAL

☐ SPIRITUAL

Date: ....

Today's self-care activity: ....

....

- ....

....

....

....

....

Choose You check-in...HOW DID I FEEL?

BEFORE:	DURING:	AFTER:
☐ CALM	☐ RELAXED	☐ HOPEFUL
☐ CHEERFUL	☐ AWESOME	☐ CONFIDENT
☐ IN CONTROL	☐ STRONG	☐ PROUD
☐ STRESSED	☐ ENERGIZED	☐ PEACEFUL
☐ DISTRACTED	☐ HAPPY	☐ GROUNDED
☐ EMOTIONAL	☐ SURPRISED	☐ FOCUSED
☐ OVERWHELMED	☐ RELIEVED	☐ CONTENT
☐ ANXIOUS	☐ FREE	☐ _____
☐ ANGRY	☐ _____	☐ _____
☐ _____	☐ _____	☐ _____
☐ _____	☐ _____	☐ _____

THIS WAS JUST WHAT I NEEDED BECAUSE...

....

....

....

....

....

....

....

....

KEEP IT GOING!

Whenever you can, start your day with self-care, even if it's quick. Making yourself a priority when you first wake up helps set the tone for the day and makes it more likely that you'll fit in additional time for yourself as your day continues.

MY AWESOME NOTES!

....

....

....

....

....

....

....

....

....

....

....

TODAY I CHOSE THIS TYPE OF SELF-CARE:

- ☐ EMOTIONAL
- ☐ MENTAL
- ☐ PHYSICAL
- ☐ PRACTICAL
- ☐ SOCIAL
- ☐ SPIRITUAL

DATE:

TODAY'S SELF-CARE ACTIVITY:

- ☐ **MAKE THIS A REGULAR ACTIVITY**
- ☐ **THIS IS GREAT FOR SPECIAL OCCASIONS**
- ☐ **GIVE THIS ANOTHER TRY ON A DIFFERENT DAY**
- ☐ **THIS ISN'T FOR ME**

CHOOSE YOU CHECK-IN...HOW DID I FEEL?

BEFORE:	DURING:	AFTER:
☐ CALM	☐ RELAXED	☐ HOPEFUL
☐ CHEERFUL	☐ AWESOME	☐ CONFIDENT
☐ IN CONTROL	☐ STRONG	☐ PROUD
☐ STRESSED	☐ ENERGIZED	☐ PEACEFUL
☐ DISTRACTED	☐ HAPPY	☐ GROUNDED
☐ EMOTIONAL	☐ SURPRISED	☐ FOCUSED
☐ OVERWHELMED	☐ RELIEVED	☐ CONTENT
☐ ANXIOUS	☐ FREE	☐ _____
☐ ANGRY	☐ _____	☐ _____
☐ _____	☐ _____	☐ _____
☐ _____	☐ _____	☐ _____

THIS WAS JUST WHAT I NEEDED BECAUSE...

FEEL-GOOD IDEAS!

If you want to do emotional and mental self-care, take stock of the people who are closest to you. Plan to spend more time with the people who fill you up and figure out how to spend less time with the people who leave you feeling depleted and empty.

MY AWESOME NOTES!

TODAY I CHOSE THIS TYPE OF SELF-CARE:

☐ EMOTIONAL

☐ MENTAL

☐ PHYSICAL

☐ PRACTICAL

☐ SOCIAL

☐ SPIRITUAL

DATE:
....

TODAY'S SELF-CARE ACTIVITY:
....
....
....
....
....
....
....

CHOOSE YOU CHECK-IN...HOW DID I FEEL?

BEFORE:
☐ CALM
☐ CHEERFUL
☐ IN CONTROL
☐ STRESSED
☐ DISTRACTED
☐ EMOTIONAL
☐ OVERWHELMED
☐ ANXIOUS
☐ ANGRY
☐ _____
☐ _____

DURING:
☐ RELAXED
☐ AWESOME
☐ STRONG
☐ ENERGIZED
☐ HAPPY
☐ SURPRISED
☐ RELIEVED
☐ FREE
☐ _____
☐ _____
☐ _____

AFTER:
☐ HOPEFUL
☐ CONFIDENT
☐ PROUD
☐ PEACEFUL
☐ GROUNDED
☐ FOCUSED
☐ CONTENT
☐ _____
☐ _____
☐ _____

THIS WAS JUST WHAT I NEEDED BECAUSE...

....

....

....

....

....

....

....

....

....

KEEP IT GOING!

Positivity is some of the best mental self-care you can give yourself! By continuously making the decision to shift away from negative thinking and focus on positive and helpful thoughts, you create a better mood and a more positive outlook on life. You also become more prepared to handle whatever life brings.

MY AWESOME NOTES!

....

....

....

....

....

....

....

....

....

....

....

TODAY I CHOSE THIS TYPE OF SELF-CARE:

☐ EMOTIONAL

☐ MENTAL

☐ PHYSICAL

☐ PRACTICAL

☐ SOCIAL

☐ SPIRITUAL

DATE:

TODAY'S SELF-CARE ACTIVITY:

- ☐ MAKE THIS A REGULAR ACTIVITY
- ☐ THIS IS GREAT FOR SPECIAL OCCASIONS
- ☐ GIVE THIS ANOTHER TRY ON A DIFFERENT DAY
- ☐ THIS ISN'T FOR ME

CHOOSE YOU CHECK-IN...HOW DID I FEEL?

BEFORE:	DURING:	AFTER:
☐ CALM	☐ RELAXED	☐ HOPEFUL
☐ CHEERFUL	☐ AWESOME	☐ CONFIDENT
☐ IN CONTROL	☐ STRONG	☐ PROUD
☐ STRESSED	☐ ENERGIZED	☐ PEACEFUL
☐ DISTRACTED	☐ HAPPY	☐ GROUNDED
☐ EMOTIONAL	☐ SURPRISED	☐ FOCUSED
☐ OVERWHELMED	☐ RELIEVED	☐ CONTENT
☐ ANXIOUS	☐ FREE	☐ _____
☐ ANGRY	☐ _____	☐ _____
☐ _____	☐ _____	☐ _____
☐ _____	☐ _____	☐ _____

THIS WAS JUST WHAT I NEEDED BECAUSE...

STAY INSPIRED!

"Almost everything will work again if you unplug it for a few minutes, including you."

−Anne Lamott, author

MY AWESOME NOTES!

TODAY I CHOSE THIS TYPE OF SELF-CARE:

☐ EMOTIONAL

☐ MENTAL

☐ PHYSICAL

☐ PRACTICAL

☐ SOCIAL

☐ SPIRITUAL

DATE: ....

TODAY'S SELF-CARE ACTIVITY: ....

....
....
....
....
....
....

TODAY'S TAKEAWAY!

☐ MAKE THIS A REGULAR ACTIVITY

☐ THIS IS GREAT FOR SPECIAL OCCASIONS

☐ GIVE THIS ANOTHER TRY ON A DIFFERENT DAY

☐ THIS ISN'T FOR ME

CHOOSE YOU CHECK-IN...HOW DID I FEEL?

BEFORE:

☐ CALM
☐ CHEERFUL
☐ IN CONTROL
☐ STRESSED
☐ DISTRACTED
☐ EMOTIONAL
☐ OVERWHELMED
☐ ANXIOUS
☐ ANGRY
☐ _____
☐ _____

DURING:

☐ RELAXED
☐ AWESOME
☐ STRONG
☐ ENERGIZED
☐ HAPPY
☐ SURPRISED
☐ RELIEVED
☐ FREE
☐ _____
☐ _____

AFTER:

☐ HOPEFUL
☐ CONFIDENT
☐ PROUD
☐ PEACEFUL
☐ GROUNDED
☐ FOCUSED
☐ CONTENT
☐ _____
☐ _____
☐ _____

THIS WAS JUST WHAT I NEEDED BECAUSE...

....

....

....

....

....

....

....

....

....

FEEL-GOOD IDEAS!

Turn on some music and dance! No judgment about your skill or rhythm—just move to the music and enjoy how your body and mind feel. Pick a song that speaks to your soul and dance from the heart, knowing that this self-care activity helps you meet your physical and emotional needs.

MY AWESOME NOTES!

....

....

....

....

....

....

....

....

....

....

....

....

TODAY I CHOSE THIS TYPE OF SELF-CARE:

☐ EMOTIONAL

☐ MENTAL

☐ PHYSICAL

☐ PRACTICAL

☐ SOCIAL

☐ SPIRITUAL

DATE: ....

TODAY'S SELF-CARE
ACTIVITY: ....

....
....
....
....
....
....

🍃 *TODAY'S*
TAKEAWAY! 🍃

☐ MAKE THIS A
  REGULAR ACTIVITY

☐ THIS IS GREAT
  FOR SPECIAL
  OCCASIONS

☐ GIVE THIS ANOTHER
  TRY ON A
  DIFFERENT DAY

☐ THIS ISN'T FOR ME

CHOOSE YOU CHECK-IN...HOW DID I FEEL?

BEFORE:	*DURING:*	*AFTER:*
☐ CALM	☐ RELAXED	☐ HOPEFUL
☐ CHEERFUL	☐ AWESOME	☐ CONFIDENT
☐ IN CONTROL	☐ STRONG	☐ PROUD
☐ STRESSED	☐ ENERGIZED	☐ PEACEFUL
☐ DISTRACTED	☐ HAPPY	☐ GROUNDED
☐ EMOTIONAL	☐ SURPRISED	☐ FOCUSED
☐ OVERWHELMED	☐ RELIEVED	☐ CONTENT
☐ ANXIOUS	☐ FREE	☐ _____
☐ ANGRY	☐ _____	☐ _____
☐ _____	☐ _____	☐ _____
☐ _____	☐ _____	☐ _____

THIS WAS JUST WHAT I NEEDED BECAUSE...

....

....

....

....

....

....

....

....

KEEP IT GOING!

Be proactive about your self-care whenever you can. Like the saying goes, you can't pour from an empty cup. Keep up with self-care even when you're busy and even if it's just for a couple of minutes at a time.

MY AWESOME NOTES!

....

....

....

....

....

....

....

....

....

....

....

TODAY I CHOSE THIS TYPE OF SELF–CARE:

☐ EMOTIONAL

☐ MENTAL

☐ PHYSICAL

☐ PRACTICAL

☐ SOCIAL

☐ SPIRITUAL

DATE:
TODAY'S SELF-CARE ACTIVITY:

- ☐ MAKE THIS A REGULAR ACTIVITY
- ☐ THIS IS GREAT FOR SPECIAL OCCASIONS
- ☐ GIVE THIS ANOTHER TRY ON A DIFFERENT DAY
- ☐ THIS ISN'T FOR ME

CHOOSE YOU CHECK-IN...HOW DID I FEEL?

BEFORE:
- ☐ CALM
- ☐ CHEERFUL
- ☐ IN CONTROL
- ☐ STRESSED
- ☐ DISTRACTED
- ☐ EMOTIONAL
- ☐ OVERWHELMED
- ☐ ANXIOUS
- ☐ ANGRY
- ☐ _____
- ☐ _____

DURING:
- ☐ RELAXED
- ☐ AWESOME
- ☐ STRONG
- ☐ ENERGIZED
- ☐ HAPPY
- ☐ SURPRISED
- ☐ RELIEVED
- ☐ FREE
- ☐ _____
- ☐ _____
- ☐ _____

AFTER:
- ☐ HOPEFUL
- ☐ CONFIDENT
- ☐ PROUD
- ☐ PEACEFUL
- ☐ GROUNDED
- ☐ FOCUSED
- ☐ CONTENT
- ☐ _____
- ☐ _____
- ☐ _____

THIS WAS JUST WHAT I NEEDED BECAUSE...

FEEL-GOOD IDEAS! Plan a get-together with friends. Depending on your preference, this can be at home, like a spa day, or you can head out for a night on the town for dinner and drinks. Aim to get this social experience on the calendar in the next few weeks!

MY AWESOME NOTES!

TODAY I CHOSE THIS TYPE OF SELF-CARE:

☐ EMOTIONAL

☐ MENTAL

☐ PHYSICAL

☐ PRACTICAL

☐ SOCIAL

☐ SPIRITUAL

DATE:

TODAY'S SELF-CARE ACTIVITY:

CHOOSE YOU CHECK-IN...HOW DID I FEEL?

BEFORE:

☐ CALM
☐ CHEERFUL
☐ IN CONTROL
☐ STRESSED
☐ DISTRACTED
☐ EMOTIONAL
☐ OVERWHELMED
☐ ANXIOUS
☐ ANGRY
☐ _____
☐ _____

DURING:

☐ RELAXED
☐ AWESOME
☐ STRONG
☐ ENERGIZED
☐ HAPPY
☐ SURPRISED
☐ RELIEVED
☐ FREE
☐ _____
☐ _____

AFTER:

☐ HOPEFUL
☐ CONFIDENT
☐ PROUD
☐ PEACEFUL
☐ GROUNDED
☐ FOCUSED
☐ CONTENT
☐ _____
☐ _____
☐ _____

THIS WAS JUST WHAT I NEEDED BECAUSE...

....

....

....

....

....

....

....

....

KEEP IT GOING!

Remember that self-care doesn't have to happen at the same time or in the same way each day. When you take the time to look ahead at your week to see where you can fit in moments for yourself, keep in mind a few minutes are better than nothing!

MY AWESOME NOTES!

....

....

....

....

....

....

....

....

....

....

....

....

TODAY I CHOSE THIS TYPE OF SELF-CARE:

☐ EMOTIONAL

☐ MENTAL

☐ PHYSICAL

☐ PRACTICAL

☐ SOCIAL

☐ SPIRITUAL

Date: ....

Today's self-care activity: ....

....
....
....
....
....

Choose You check-in... HOW DID I FEEL?

BEFORE:	DURING:	AFTER:
☐ CALM	☐ RELAXED	☐ HOPEFUL
☐ CHEERFUL	☐ AWESOME	☐ CONFIDENT
☐ IN CONTROL	☐ STRONG	☐ PROUD
☐ STRESSED	☐ ENERGIZED	☐ PEACEFUL
☐ DISTRACTED	☐ HAPPY	☐ GROUNDED
☐ EMOTIONAL	☐ SURPRISED	☐ FOCUSED
☐ OVERWHELMED	☐ RELIEVED	☐ CONTENT
☐ ANXIOUS	☐ FREE	☐ _____
☐ ANGRY	☐ _____	☐ _____
☐ _____	☐ _____	☐ _____
☐ _____	☐ _____	☐ _____

THIS WAS JUST WHAT I NEEDED BECAUSE...

....

....

....

....

....

....

....

....

MY AWESOME NOTES!

....

....

....

....

....

....

....

....

....

....

TODAY I CHOSE THIS TYPE OF SELF-CARE:

☐ EMOTIONAL

☐ MENTAL

☐ PHYSICAL

☐ PRACTICAL

☐ SOCIAL

☐ SPIRITUAL

DATE: ....

TODAY'S SELF-CARE ACTIVITY: ....

....
....
....
....
....
....

- ☐ MAKE THIS A REGULAR ACTIVITY
- ☐ THIS IS GREAT FOR SPECIAL OCCASIONS
- ☐ GIVE THIS ANOTHER TRY ON A DIFFERENT DAY
- ☐ THIS ISN'T FOR ME

CHOOSE YOU CHECK-IN...HOW DID I FEEL?

BEFORE:	DURING:	AFTER:
☐ CALM	☐ RELAXED	☐ HOPEFUL
☐ CHEERFUL	☐ AWESOME	☐ CONFIDENT
☐ IN CONTROL	☐ STRONG	☐ PROUD
☐ STRESSED	☐ ENERGIZED	☐ PEACEFUL
☐ DISTRACTED	☐ HAPPY	☐ GROUNDED
☐ EMOTIONAL	☐ SURPRISED	☐ FOCUSED
☐ OVERWHELMED	☐ RELIEVED	☐ CONTENT
☐ ANXIOUS	☐ FREE	☐ _____
☐ ANGRY	☐ _____	☐ _____
☐ _____	☐ _____	☐ _____
☐ _____	☐ _____	☐ _____

THIS WAS JUST WHAT I NEEDED BECAUSE...

....

....

....

....

....

....

....

....

MY AWESOME NOTES!

....

....

....

....

....

....

....

....

....

....

TODAY I CHOSE THIS TYPE OF SELF-CARE:

- ☐ EMOTIONAL
- ☐ MENTAL
- ☐ PHYSICAL
- ☐ PRACTICAL
- ☐ SOCIAL
- ☐ SPIRITUAL

DATE: ....

*TODAY'S SELF-CARE
ACTIVITY:* ....

....

....

....

....

....

....

TODAY'S TAKEAWAY!

- ☐ **MAKE THIS A REGULAR ACTIVITY**
- ☐ **THIS IS GREAT FOR SPECIAL OCCASIONS**
- ☐ **GIVE THIS ANOTHER TRY ON A DIFFERENT DAY**
- ☐ **THIS ISN'T FOR ME**

CHOOSE YOU CHECK-IN...HOW DID I FEEL?

BEFORE:

- ☐ **CALM**
- ☐ **CHEERFUL**
- ☐ **IN CONTROL**
- ☐ **STRESSED**
- ☐ **DISTRACTED**
- ☐ **EMOTIONAL**
- ☐ **OVERWHELMED**
- ☐ **ANXIOUS**
- ☐ **ANGRY**
- ☐ _____
- ☐ _____

DURING:

- ☐ **RELAXED**
- ☐ **AWESOME**
- ☐ **STRONG**
- ☐ **ENERGIZED**
- ☐ **HAPPY**
- ☐ **SURPRISED**
- ☐ **RELIEVED**
- ☐ **FREE**
- ☐ _____
- ☐ _____
- ☐ _____

AFTER:

- ☐ **HOPEFUL**
- ☐ **CONFIDENT**
- ☐ **PROUD**
- ☐ **PEACEFUL**
- ☐ **GROUNDED**
- ☐ **FOCUSED**
- ☐ **CONTENT**
- ☐ _____
- ☐ _____
- ☐ _____

THIS WAS JUST WHAT I NEEDED BECAUSE...

....

....

....

....

....

....

....

KEEP IT GOING! Self-care can be both planned and spontaneous! Maybe you didn't plan to take an hour to watch TV. Or maybe you spontaneously ran into a friend at the coffee shop and stopped to chat for a while. Take notice of these surprise moments as important self-care activities.

MY AWESOME NOTES!

....

....

....

....

....

....

....

....

....

....

....

TODAY I CHOSE THIS TYPE OF SELF-CARE:

☐ EMOTIONAL

☐ MENTAL

☐ PHYSICAL

☐ PRACTICAL

☐ SOCIAL

☐ SPIRITUAL

DATE: ....

TODAY'S SELF-CARE ACTIVITY: ....

....
....
....
....
....
....

☐ MAKE THIS A REGULAR ACTIVITY

☐ THIS IS GREAT FOR SPECIAL OCCASIONS

☐ GIVE THIS ANOTHER TRY ON A DIFFERENT DAY

☐ THIS ISN'T FOR ME

CHOOSE YOU CHECK-IN...HOW DID I FEEL?

BEFORE:

☐ CALM
☐ CHEERFUL
☐ IN CONTROL
☐ STRESSED
☐ DISTRACTED
☐ EMOTIONAL
☐ OVERWHELMED
☐ ANXIOUS
☐ ANGRY
☐ _____
☐ _____

DURING:

☐ RELAXED
☐ AWESOME
☐ STRONG
☐ ENERGIZED
☐ HAPPY
☐ SURPRISED
☐ RELIEVED
☐ FREE
☐ _____
☐ _____

AFTER:

☐ HOPEFUL
☐ CONFIDENT
☐ PROUD
☐ PEACEFUL
☐ GROUNDED
☐ FOCUSED
☐ CONTENT
☐ _____
☐ _____
☐ _____
☐ _____

THIS WAS JUST WHAT I NEEDED BECAUSE...

FEEL-GOOD IDEAS!

Get cozy! Put on your most comfy clothes or jammies, curl up in a blanket, and sit in a spot that's comfortable. Add some relaxing music or candles, meditate, or simply sit and breathe to connect with your spiritual self.

MY AWESOME NOTES!

TODAY I CHOSE THIS TYPE OF SELF-CARE:

- ☐ EMOTIONAL
- ☐ MENTAL
- ☐ PHYSICAL
- ☐ PRACTICAL
- ☐ SOCIAL
- ☐ SPIRITUAL

Date: ....
Today's self-care activity: ....
....
....
....
....
....
....

☐ MAKE THIS A REGULAR ACTIVITY

☐ THIS IS GREAT FOR SPECIAL OCCASIONS

☐ GIVE THIS ANOTHER TRY ON A DIFFERENT DAY

☐ THIS ISN'T FOR ME

Choose You check-in...HOW DID I FEEL?

BEFORE:	DURING:	AFTER:
☐ CALM	☐ RELAXED	☐ HOPEFUL
☐ CHEERFUL	☐ AWESOME	☐ CONFIDENT
☐ IN CONTROL	☐ STRONG	☐ PROUD
☐ STRESSED	☐ ENERGIZED	☐ PEACEFUL
☐ DISTRACTED	☐ HAPPY	☐ GROUNDED
☐ EMOTIONAL	☐ SURPRISED	☐ FOCUSED
☐ OVERWHELMED	☐ RELIEVED	☐ CONTENT
☐ ANXIOUS	☐ FREE	☐ _____
☐ ANGRY	☐ _____	☐ _____
☐ _____	☐ _____	☐ _____
☐ _____	☐ _____	☐ _____

THIS WAS JUST WHAT I NEEDED BECAUSE...

STAY INSPIRED!

"Self-care is not selfish or self-indulgent. We cannot nurture others from a dry well. We need to take care of our own needs first, then we can give from our surplus, our abundance."

—Jennifer Louden, author

MY AWESOME NOTES!

TODAY I CHOSE THIS TYPE OF SELF-CARE:

- ☐ EMOTIONAL
- ☐ MENTAL
- ☐ PHYSICAL
- ☐ PRACTICAL
- ☐ SOCIAL
- ☐ SPIRITUAL

Date: ....

Today's self-care activity: ....

....

....

....

....

....

☐ MAKE THIS A REGULAR ACTIVITY

☐ THIS IS GREAT FOR SPECIAL OCCASIONS

☐ GIVE THIS ANOTHER TRY ON A DIFFERENT DAY

☐ THIS ISN'T FOR ME

Choose You check-in...How did I feel?

BEFORE:

☐ CALM
☐ CHEERFUL
☐ IN CONTROL
☐ STRESSED
☐ DISTRACTED
☐ EMOTIONAL
☐ OVERWHELMED
☐ ANXIOUS
☐ ANGRY
☐ _____
☐ _____

DURING:

☐ RELAXED
☐ AWESOME
☐ STRONG
☐ ENERGIZED
☐ HAPPY
☐ SURPRISED
☐ RELIEVED
☐ FREE
☐ _____
☐ _____
☐ _____

AFTER:

☐ HOPEFUL
☐ CONFIDENT
☐ PROUD
☐ PEACEFUL
☐ GROUNDED
☐ FOCUSED
☐ CONTENT
☐ _____
☐ _____
☐ _____

THIS WAS JUST WHAT I NEEDED BECAUSE...

....
....
....
....
....
....
....

FEEL-GOOD IDEAS!

Go for a walk with a friend or loved one. Using your body, connecting with someone, and getting out into nature give your body, mind, and spirit self-care! Even better, make walks a regular habit, on your own or with a friend.

MY AWESOME NOTES!

....
....
....
....
....
....
....
....
....
....

TODAY I CHOSE THIS TYPE OF SELF-CARE:

☐ EMOTIONAL

☐ MENTAL

☐ PHYSICAL

☐ PRACTICAL

☐ SOCIAL

☐ SPIRITUAL

Date: ....

Today's self-care activity: ....

....

....

....

....

....

....

Choose You check-in...how did I feel?

BEFORE:	DURING:	AFTER:
☐ CALM	☐ RELAXED	☐ HOPEFUL
☐ CHEERFUL	☐ AWESOME	☐ CONFIDENT
☐ IN CONTROL	☐ STRONG	☐ PROUD
☐ STRESSED	☐ ENERGIZED	☐ PEACEFUL
☐ DISTRACTED	☐ HAPPY	☐ GROUNDED
☐ EMOTIONAL	☐ SURPRISED	☐ FOCUSED
☐ OVERWHELMED	☐ RELIEVED	☐ CONTENT
☐ ANXIOUS	☐ FREE	☐ _____
☐ ANGRY	☐ _____	☐ _____
☐ _____	☐ _____	☐ _____
☐ _____	☐ _____	☐ _____

THIS WAS JUST WHAT I NEEDED BECAUSE...

....

....

....

....

....

....

....

....

KEEP IT GOING! Self-care has a cumulative effect. When you make yourself a priority on a regular basis, even in small ways, you'll likely start to notice positive changes in how you're thinking and feeling. And when you think and feel more positively, you're sure to notice a favorable impact on how you experience life.

MY AWESOME NOTES!

....

....

....

....

....

....

....

....

....

....

TODAY I CHOSE THIS TYPE OF SELF–CARE:

☐ EMOTIONAL

☐ MENTAL

☐ PHYSICAL

☐ PRACTICAL

☐ SOCIAL

☐ SPIRITUAL

DATE:

TODAY'S SELF-CARE ACTIVITY:

- ☐ MAKE THIS A REGULAR ACTIVITY
- ☐ THIS IS GREAT FOR SPECIAL OCCASIONS
- ☐ GIVE THIS ANOTHER TRY ON A DIFFERENT DAY
- ☐ THIS ISN'T FOR ME

CHOOSE YOU CHECK-IN...HOW DID I FEEL?

BEFORE:	DURING:	AFTER:
☐ CALM	☐ RELAXED	☐ HOPEFUL
☐ CHEERFUL	☐ AWESOME	☐ CONFIDENT
☐ IN CONTROL	☐ STRONG	☐ PROUD
☐ STRESSED	☐ ENERGIZED	☐ PEACEFUL
☐ DISTRACTED	☐ HAPPY	☐ GROUNDED
☐ EMOTIONAL	☐ SURPRISED	☐ FOCUSED
☐ OVERWHELMED	☐ RELIEVED	☐ CONTENT
☐ ANXIOUS	☐ FREE	☐ _____
☐ ANGRY	☐ _____	☐ _____
☐ _____	☐ _____	☐ _____
☐ _____	☐ _____	☐ _____

THIS WAS JUST WHAT I NEEDED BECAUSE...

....

....

....

....

....

....

....

....

....

FEEL-GOOD IDEAS!

Sit and breathe deeply. Find a quiet space, sit or lie comfortably, and follow the natural rhythm of your breath. Then slow down your breathing, inhaling and exhaling deeply. Focus on your breath and allow your mind to become quiet, creating room for more calm, clarity, and mental self-care.

MY AWESOME NOTES!

....

....

....

....

....

....

....

....

....

....

....

TODAY I CHOSE THIS TYPE OF SELF-CARE:

☐ EMOTIONAL

☐ MENTAL

☐ PHYSICAL

☐ PRACTICAL

☐ SOCIAL

☐ SPIRITUAL

DATE: ....

TODAY'S SELF-CARE ACTIVITY: ....

....

....

....

....

....

....

CHOOSE YOU CHECK-IN...HOW DID I FEEL?

BEFORE:	DURING:	AFTER:
☐ CALM	☐ RELAXED	☐ HOPEFUL
☐ CHEERFUL	☐ AWESOME	☐ CONFIDENT
☐ IN CONTROL	☐ STRONG	☐ PROUD
☐ STRESSED	☐ ENERGIZED	☐ PEACEFUL
☐ DISTRACTED	☐ HAPPY	☐ GROUNDED
☐ EMOTIONAL	☐ SURPRISED	☐ FOCUSED
☐ OVERWHELMED	☐ RELIEVED	☐ CONTENT
☐ ANXIOUS	☐ FREE	☐ _____
☐ ANGRY	☐ _____	☐ _____
☐ _____	☐ _____	☐ _____
☐ _____	☐ _____	☐ _____

THIS WAS JUST WHAT I NEEDED BECAUSE...

MY AWESOME NOTES!

TODAY I CHOSE THIS TYPE OF SELF-CARE:

☐ EMOTIONAL

☐ MENTAL

☐ PHYSICAL

☐ PRACTICAL

☐ SOCIAL

☐ SPIRITUAL

Date:

Today's self-care activity:

Choose You Check-in...How did I feel?

BEFORE:	DURING:	AFTER:
☐ CALM	☐ RELAXED	☐ HOPEFUL
☐ CHEERFUL	☐ AWESOME	☐ CONFIDENT
☐ IN CONTROL	☐ STRONG	☐ PROUD
☐ STRESSED	☐ ENERGIZED	☐ PEACEFUL
☐ DISTRACTED	☐ HAPPY	☐ GROUNDED
☐ EMOTIONAL	☐ SURPRISED	☐ FOCUSED
☐ OVERWHELMED	☐ RELIEVED	☐ CONTENT
☐ ANXIOUS	☐ FREE	☐ _____
☐ ANGRY	☐ _____	☐ _____
☐ _____	☐ _____	☐ _____
☐ _____		

THIS WAS JUST WHAT I NEEDED BECAUSE...

....

....

....

....

....

....

....

....

KEEP IT GOING!

There is no shame in getting support. Self-care is taking care of yourself, and sometimes you also need someone else, possibly a professional, to assist with this. Whether that's a nutritionist, personal trainer, therapist, or another pro, reach out and accept help. You deserve it!

MY AWESOME NOTES!

....

....

....

....

....

....

....

....

....

....

....

....

TODAY I CHOSE THIS TYPE OF SELF-CARE:

☐ EMOTIONAL

☐ MENTAL

☐ PHYSICAL

☐ PRACTICAL

☐ SOCIAL

☐ SPIRITUAL

*D*ATE: ....

*T*ODAY'S SELF-CARE
ACTIVITY: ....

....

....

....

....

....

....

TODAY'S TAKEAWAY!

☐ MAKE THIS A REGULAR ACTIVITY

☐ THIS IS GREAT FOR SPECIAL OCCASIONS

☐ GIVE THIS ANOTHER TRY ON A DIFFERENT DAY

☐ THIS ISN'T FOR ME

*C*HOOSE *Y*OU CHECK-IN...HOW DID I FEEL?

BEFORE:	DURING:	AFTER:
☐ CALM	☐ RELAXED	☐ HOPEFUL
☐ CHEERFUL	☐ AWESOME	☐ CONFIDENT
☐ IN CONTROL	☐ STRONG	☐ PROUD
☐ STRESSED	☐ ENERGIZED	☐ PEACEFUL
☐ DISTRACTED	☐ HAPPY	☐ GROUNDED
☐ EMOTIONAL	☐ SURPRISED	☐ FOCUSED
☐ OVERWHELMED	☐ RELIEVED	☐ CONTENT
☐ ANXIOUS	☐ FREE	☐ _____
☐ ANGRY	☐ _____	☐ _____
☐ _____	☐ _____	☐ _____
☐ _____	☐ _____	☐ _____

THIS WAS JUST WHAT I NEEDED BECAUSE...

FEEL-GOOD IDEAS!

Have a movie night, either on your own or with someone else. Watch movies that make you feel good, indulge in a treat or two, and enjoy. Creating positive emotions is an important part of your self-care.

MY AWESOME NOTES!

TODAY I CHOSE THIS TYPE OF SELF-CARE:

- ☐ EMOTIONAL
- ☐ MENTAL
- ☐ PHYSICAL
- ☐ PRACTICAL
- ☐ SOCIAL
- ☐ SPIRITUAL

DATE: ....

TODAY'S SELF-CARE ACTIVITY: ....

....

....

....

....

....

....

🍃 TODAY'S 🍃
TAKEAWAY!

☐ MAKE THIS A REGULAR ACTIVITY

☐ THIS IS GREAT FOR SPECIAL OCCASIONS

☐ GIVE THIS ANOTHER TRY ON A DIFFERENT DAY

☐ THIS ISN'T FOR ME

CHOOSE YOU CHECK-IN...HOW DID I FEEL?

BEFORE:	DURING:	AFTER:
☐ CALM	☐ RELAXED	☐ HOPEFUL
☐ CHEERFUL	☐ AWESOME	☐ CONFIDENT
☐ IN CONTROL	☐ STRONG	☐ PROUD
☐ STRESSED	☐ ENERGIZED	☐ PEACEFUL
☐ DISTRACTED	☐ HAPPY	☐ GROUNDED
☐ EMOTIONAL	☐ SURPRISED	☐ FOCUSED
☐ OVERWHELMED	☐ RELIEVED	☐ CONTENT
☐ ANXIOUS	☐ FREE	☐ _____
☐ ANGRY	☐ _____	☐ _____
☐ _____	☐ _____	☐ _____
☐ _____	☐ _____	☐ _____

THIS WAS JUST WHAT I NEEDED BECAUSE...

....
....
....
....
....
....
....
....

KEEP IT GOING!
Self-care
and balance
influence each other. If
you want to feel more balance
in your life, try adding in more
self-care and see if that helps.
Make more time for yourself
and notice if your feelings of
(un)balance start to shift.

MY AWESOME NOTES!

....
....
....
....
....
....
....
....
....
....
....

TODAY I CHOSE THIS TYPE OF SELF-CARE:

☐ EMOTIONAL

☐ MENTAL

☐ PHYSICAL

☐ PRACTICAL

☐ SOCIAL

☐ SPIRITUAL

Date: ....

Today's self-care activity: ....
....
....
....
....
....
....

☐ **MAKE THIS A REGULAR ACTIVITY**

☐ **THIS IS GREAT FOR SPECIAL OCCASIONS**

☐ **GIVE THIS ANOTHER TRY ON A DIFFERENT DAY**

☐ **THIS ISN'T FOR ME**

Choose You check-in...HOW DID I FEEL?

BEFORE:	*DURING:*	*AFTER:*
☐ CALM	☐ RELAXED	☐ HOPEFUL
☐ CHEERFUL	☐ AWESOME	☐ CONFIDENT
☐ IN CONTROL	☐ STRONG	☐ PROUD
☐ STRESSED	☐ ENERGIZED	☐ PEACEFUL
☐ DISTRACTED	☐ HAPPY	☐ GROUNDED
☐ EMOTIONAL	☐ SURPRISED	☐ FOCUSED
☐ OVERWHELMED	☐ RELIEVED	☐ CONTENT
☐ ANXIOUS	☐ FREE	☐ _____
☐ ANGRY	☐ _____	☐ _____
☐ _____	☐ _____	☐ _____
☐ _____	☐ _____	☐ _____

THIS WAS JUST WHAT I NEEDED BECAUSE...

FEEL-GOOD IDEAS!

Give yoga or Pilates a try. Both are great for body, mind, and soul. Websites like YouTube have a large selection of videos for practitioners of every level. If you're just starting out, remember that everyone is a beginner at some point, and focus on the experience rather than on how you're doing.

MY AWESOME NOTES!

TODAY I CHOSE THIS TYPE OF SELF-CARE:

- ☐ EMOTIONAL
- ☐ MENTAL
- ☐ PHYSICAL
- ☐ PRACTICAL
- ☐ SOCIAL
- ☐ SPIRITUAL

DATE:

TODAY'S SELF-CARE ACTIVITY:

....

....

....

....

....

....

....

TODAY'S —— —— TAKEAWAY!

☐ MAKE THIS A REGULAR ACTIVITY

☐ THIS IS GREAT FOR SPECIAL OCCASIONS

☐ GIVE THIS ANOTHER TRY ON A DIFFERENT DAY

☐ THIS ISN'T FOR ME

CHOOSE YOU CHECK-IN... HOW DID I FEEL?

BEFORE:

☐ CALM
☐ CHEERFUL
☐ IN CONTROL
☐ STRESSED
☐ DISTRACTED
☐ EMOTIONAL
☐ OVERWHELMED
☐ ANXIOUS
☐ ANGRY
☐ _____
☐ _____

DURING:

☐ RELAXED
☐ AWESOME
☐ STRONG
☐ ENERGIZED
☐ HAPPY
☐ SURPRISED
☐ RELIEVED
☐ FREE
☐ _____
☐ _____
☐ _____

AFTER:

☐ HOPEFUL
☐ CONFIDENT
☐ PROUD
☐ PEACEFUL
☐ GROUNDED
☐ FOCUSED
☐ CONTENT
☐ _____
☐ _____
☐ _____

THIS WAS JUST WHAT I NEEDED BECAUSE...

....

....

....

....

....

....

....

....

MY AWESOME NOTES!

....

....

....

....

....

....

....

....

....

....

....

TODAY I CHOSE THIS TYPE OF SELF-CARE:

☐ EMOTIONAL

☐ MENTAL

☐ PHYSICAL

☐ PRACTICAL

☐ SOCIAL

☐ SPIRITUAL

DATE: ....

TODAY'S SELF-CARE
ACTIVITY: ....

....

....

....

....

....

....

TODAY'S TAKEAWAY!

- ☐ **MAKE THIS A REGULAR ACTIVITY**
- ☐ **THIS IS GREAT FOR SPECIAL OCCASIONS**
- ☐ **GIVE THIS ANOTHER TRY ON A DIFFERENT DAY**
- ☐ **THIS ISN'T FOR ME**

CHOOSE YOU CHECK-IN...HOW DID I FEEL?

BEFORE:	DURING:	AFTER:
☐ CALM	☐ RELAXED	☐ HOPEFUL
☐ CHEERFUL	☐ AWESOME	☐ CONFIDENT
☐ IN CONTROL	☐ STRONG	☐ PROUD
☐ STRESSED	☐ ENERGIZED	☐ PEACEFUL
☐ DISTRACTED	☐ HAPPY	☐ GROUNDED
☐ EMOTIONAL	☐ SURPRISED	☐ FOCUSED
☐ OVERWHELMED	☐ RELIEVED	☐ CONTENT
☐ ANXIOUS	☐ FREE	☐ _____
☐ ANGRY	☐ _____	☐ _____
☐ _____	☐ _____	☐ _____
☐ _____	☐ _____	

THIS WAS JUST WHAT I NEEDED BECAUSE...

....

....

....

....

....

....

....

....

....

KEEP IT GOING! Keep an eye on sale sites like *Groupon* and *LivingSocial*. They have fantastic deals on local self-care activities like massages and other spa services, exercise classes, and personal splurges like horseback riding. You can even purchase things like hair and beauty products, home spa essentials, and more.

MY AWESOME NOTES!

....

....

....

....

....

....

....

....

....

....

....

....

TODAY I CHOSE THIS TYPE OF SELF-CARE:

☐ EMOTIONAL

☐ MENTAL

☐ PHYSICAL

☐ PRACTICAL

☐ SOCIAL

☐ SPIRITUAL

*D*ATE: ....

*T*ODAY'S SELF—CARE
ACTIVITY: ....

....

....

....

....

....

....

TODAY'S TAKEAWAY!

☐ **MAKE THIS A REGULAR ACTIVITY**

☐ **THIS IS GREAT FOR SPECIAL OCCASIONS**

☐ **GIVE THIS ANOTHER TRY ON A DIFFERENT DAY**

☐ **THIS ISN'T FOR ME**

*C*HOOSE *Y*OU CHECK-IN...**HOW DID I FEEL?**

BEFORE:	DURING:	AFTER:
☐ CALM	☐ RELAXED	☐ HOPEFUL
☐ CHEERFUL	☐ AWESOME	☐ CONFIDENT
☐ IN CONTROL	☐ STRONG	☐ PROUD
☐ STRESSED	☐ ENERGIZED	☐ PEACEFUL
☐ DISTRACTED	☐ HAPPY	☐ GROUNDED
☐ EMOTIONAL	☐ SURPRISED	☐ FOCUSED
☐ OVERWHELMED	☐ RELIEVED	☐ CONTENT
☐ ANXIOUS	☐ FREE	☐ _____
☐ ANGRY	☐ _____	☐ _____
☐ _____	☐ _____	☐ _____
☐ _____	☐ _____	☐ _____

THIS WAS JUST WHAT I NEEDED BECAUSE...

FEEL-GOOD IDEAS!

Have a virtual coffee date! Make plans with a friend who lives too far away to see in person and video chat while you sip coffee at home and catch up. Time and distance don't need to get in the way of social self-care!

MY AWESOME NOTES!

TODAY I CHOSE THIS TYPE OF SELF-CARE:

- ☐ EMOTIONAL
- ☐ MENTAL
- ☐ PHYSICAL
- ☐ PRACTICAL
- ☐ SOCIAL
- ☐ SPIRITUAL

DATE:

TODAY'S SELF-CARE ACTIVITY:

CHOOSE YOU CHECK-IN...HOW DID I FEEL?

BEFORE:

☐ CALM
☐ CHEERFUL
☐ IN CONTROL
☐ STRESSED
☐ DISTRACTED
☐ EMOTIONAL
☐ OVERWHELMED
☐ ANXIOUS
☐ ANGRY
☐ _____
☐ _____

DURING:

☐ RELAXED
☐ AWESOME
☐ STRONG
☐ ENERGIZED
☐ HAPPY
☐ SURPRISED
☐ RELIEVED
☐ FREE
☐ _____
☐ _____
☐ _____

AFTER:

☐ HOPEFUL
☐ CONFIDENT
☐ PROUD
☐ PEACEFUL
☐ GROUNDED
☐ FOCUSED
☐ CONTENT
☐ _____
☐ _____
☐ _____

THIS WAS JUST WHAT I NEEDED BECAUSE...

....
....
....
....
....
....
....
....

KEEP IT GOING! Be aware that others may question how much time you spend on self-care. If that happens, calmly educate them about why self-care is important and how you make the time to prioritize self-care. Chances are that the people who question are the ones who need more self-care in their own lives.

MY AWESOME NOTES!

....
....
....
....
....
....
....
....
....
....

TODAY I CHOSE THIS TYPE OF SELF–CARE:

☐ EMOTIONAL

☐ MENTAL

☐ PHYSICAL

☐ PRACTICAL

☐ SOCIAL

☐ SPIRITUAL

DATE: ....

TODAY'S SELF-CARE ACTIVITY: ....

....
....
....
....
....
....

☐ MAKE THIS A REGULAR ACTIVITY

☐ THIS IS GREAT FOR SPECIAL OCCASIONS

☐ GIVE THIS ANOTHER TRY ON A DIFFERENT DAY

☐ THIS ISN'T FOR ME

CHOOSE YOU CHECK-IN...HOW DID I FEEL?

BEFORE:

☐ CALM
☐ CHEERFUL
☐ IN CONTROL
☐ STRESSED
☐ DISTRACTED
☐ EMOTIONAL
☐ OVERWHELMED
☐ ANXIOUS
☐ ANGRY
☐ _____
☐ _____

DURING:

☐ RELAXED
☐ AWESOME
☐ STRONG
☐ ENERGIZED
☐ HAPPY
☐ SURPRISED
☐ RELIEVED
☐ FREE
☐ _____
☐ _____
☐ _____

AFTER:

☐ HOPEFUL
☐ CONFIDENT
☐ PROUD
☐ PEACEFUL
☐ GROUNDED
☐ FOCUSED
☐ CONTENT
☐ _____
☐ _____
☐ _____
☐ _____

THIS WAS JUST WHAT I NEEDED BECAUSE...

....

....

....

....

....

....

....

....

....

FEEL-GOOD IDEAS!

Your yearly doctors' appointments (annual physical, pap, dentist, etc.) are an important part of your practical and physical self-care. Make them a priority! Take the time to set these appointments for the next year or create reminders to schedule them as the time gets closer.

MY AWESOME NOTES!

....

....

....

....

....

....

....

....

....

....

TODAY I CHOSE THIS TYPE OF SELF-CARE:

☐ EMOTIONAL

☐ MENTAL

☐ PHYSICAL

☐ PRACTICAL

☐ SOCIAL

☐ SPIRITUAL

DATE: ....

TODAY'S SELF-CARE ACTIVITY: ....

....

....

....

....

....

....

CHOOSE YOU CHECK-IN...HOW DID I FEEL?

BEFORE:	DURING:	AFTER:
☐ CALM	☐ RELAXED	☐ HOPEFUL
☐ CHEERFUL	☐ AWESOME	☐ CONFIDENT
☐ IN CONTROL	☐ STRONG	☐ PROUD
☐ STRESSED	☐ ENERGIZED	☐ PEACEFUL
☐ DISTRACTED	☐ HAPPY	☐ GROUNDED
☐ EMOTIONAL	☐ SURPRISED	☐ FOCUSED
☐ OVERWHELMED	☐ RELIEVED	☐ CONTENT
☐ ANXIOUS	☐ FREE	☐ _____
☐ ANGRY	☐ _____	☐ _____
☐ _____	☐ _____	☐ _____
☐ _____	☐ _____	☐ _____

THIS WAS JUST WHAT I NEEDED BECAUSE...

STAY INSPIRED!

"My mission, should I choose to accept it, is to find peace with exactly who and what I am. To take pride in my thoughts, my appearance, my talents, my flaws and to stop this incessant worrying that I can't be loved as I am."

—Anaïs Nin, author

MY AWESOME NOTES!

TODAY I CHOSE THIS TYPE OF SELF-CARE:

☐ EMOTIONAL

☐ MENTAL

☐ PHYSICAL

☐ PRACTICAL

☐ SOCIAL

☐ SPIRITUAL

DATE: ....

*TODAY'S SELF—CARE
ACTIVITY:* ....

....

....

....

....

....

....

🍃 *TODAY'S
TAKEAWAY!* 🍃

☐ **MAKE THIS A
REGULAR ACTIVITY**

☐ **THIS IS GREAT
FOR SPECIAL
OCCASIONS**

☐ **GIVE THIS ANOTHER
TRY ON A
DIFFERENT DAY**

☐ **THIS ISN'T FOR ME**

CHOOSE YOU CHECK-IN...HOW DID I FEEL?

BEFORE:	*DURING:*	*AFTER:*
☐ CALM	☐ RELAXED	☐ HOPEFUL
☐ CHEERFUL	☐ AWESOME	☐ CONFIDENT
☐ IN CONTROL	☐ STRONG	☐ PROUD
☐ STRESSED	☐ ENERGIZED	☐ PEACEFUL
☐ DISTRACTED	☐ HAPPY	☐ GROUNDED
☐ EMOTIONAL	☐ SURPRISED	☐ FOCUSED
☐ OVERWHELMED	☐ RELIEVED	☐ CONTENT
☐ ANXIOUS	☐ FREE	☐ _____
☐ ANGRY	☐ _____	☐ _____
☐ _____	☐ _____	☐ _____
☐ _____	☐ _____	

THIS WAS JUST WHAT I NEEDED BECAUSE...

....
....
....
....
....
....
....
....

KEEP IT GOING! It's the intention behind the activity that can turn a task into self-care. Your morning coffee can become quiet time to yourself, or a rushed shower can become one critical minute to feel refreshed. Change your intention and find self-care activities in surprising places.

MY AWESOME NOTES!

....
....
....
....
....
....
....
....
....
....
....

TODAY I CHOSE THIS TYPE OF SELF-CARE:

☐ EMOTIONAL

☐ MENTAL

☐ PHYSICAL

☐ PRACTICAL

☐ SOCIAL

☐ SPIRITUAL

DATE:

TODAY'S SELF-CARE ACTIVITY:

- ☐ MAKE THIS A REGULAR ACTIVITY
- ☐ THIS IS GREAT FOR SPECIAL OCCASIONS
- ☐ GIVE THIS ANOTHER TRY ON A DIFFERENT DAY
- ☐ THIS ISN'T FOR ME

CHOOSE YOU CHECK-IN...HOW DID I FEEL?

BEFORE:

- ☐ CALM
- ☐ CHEERFUL
- ☐ IN CONTROL
- ☐ STRESSED
- ☐ DISTRACTED
- ☐ EMOTIONAL
- ☐ OVERWHELMED
- ☐ ANXIOUS
- ☐ ANGRY
- ☐ _____
- ☐ _____

DURING:

- ☐ RELAXED
- ☐ AWESOME
- ☐ STRONG
- ☐ ENERGIZED
- ☐ HAPPY
- ☐ SURPRISED
- ☐ RELIEVED
- ☐ FREE
- ☐ _____
- ☐ _____
- ☐ _____

AFTER:

- ☐ HOPEFUL
- ☐ CONFIDENT
- ☐ PROUD
- ☐ PEACEFUL
- ☐ GROUNDED
- ☐ FOCUSED
- ☐ CONTENT
- ☐ _____
- ☐ _____
- ☐ _____

THIS WAS JUST WHAT I NEEDED BECAUSE...

....

....

....

....

....

....

....

....

KEEP IT GOING!

Even if you don't notice an immediate positive change from self-care, keep at it! When you continually make time for self-care, you'll eventually realize you're better off than you were. You'll feel more like yourself, and you'll realize that self-care helps, even when it doesn't feel like it.

MY AWESOME NOTES!

....

....

....

....

....

....

....

....

....

....

....

TODAY I CHOSE THIS TYPE OF SELF—CARE:

☐ EMOTIONAL

☐ MENTAL

☐ PHYSICAL

☐ PRACTICAL

☐ SOCIAL

☐ SPIRITUAL

DATE:

TODAY'S SELF-CARE ACTIVITY:

TODAY'S — — TAKEAWAY!

- ☐ MAKE THIS A REGULAR ACTIVITY
- ☐ THIS IS GREAT FOR SPECIAL OCCASIONS
- ☐ GIVE THIS ANOTHER TRY ON A DIFFERENT DAY
- ☐ THIS ISN'T FOR ME

CHOOSE YOU CHECK-IN... HOW DID I FEEL?

BEFORE:	DURING:	AFTER:
☐ CALM	☐ RELAXED	☐ HOPEFUL
☐ CHEERFUL	☐ AWESOME	☐ CONFIDENT
☐ IN CONTROL	☐ STRONG	☐ PROUD
☐ STRESSED	☐ ENERGIZED	☐ PEACEFUL
☐ DISTRACTED	☐ HAPPY	☐ GROUNDED
☐ EMOTIONAL	☐ SURPRISED	☐ FOCUSED
☐ OVERWHELMED	☐ RELIEVED	☐ CONTENT
☐ ANXIOUS	☐ FREE	☐ _____
☐ ANGRY	☐ _____	☐ _____
☐ _____	☐ _____	☐ _____
☐ _____	☐ _____	☐ _____

THIS WAS JUST WHAT I NEEDED BECAUSE...

MY AWESOME NOTES!

TODAY I CHOSE THIS TYPE OF SELF-CARE:

☐ EMOTIONAL

☐ MENTAL

☐ PHYSICAL

☐ PRACTICAL

☐ SOCIAL

☐ SPIRITUAL

Date:

Today's self-care activity:

....

....

....

....

....

....

TODAY'S TAKEAWAY!

☐ MAKE THIS A REGULAR ACTIVITY

☐ THIS IS GREAT FOR SPECIAL OCCASIONS

☐ GIVE THIS ANOTHER TRY ON A DIFFERENT DAY

☐ THIS ISN'T FOR ME

Choose You check-in...How did I feel?

BEFORE:	DURING:	AFTER:
☐ CALM	☐ RELAXED	☐ HOPEFUL
☐ CHEERFUL	☐ AWESOME	☐ CONFIDENT
☐ IN CONTROL	☐ STRONG	☐ PROUD
☐ STRESSED	☐ ENERGIZED	☐ PEACEFUL
☐ DISTRACTED	☐ HAPPY	☐ GROUNDED
☐ EMOTIONAL	☐ SURPRISED	☐ FOCUSED
☐ OVERWHELMED	☐ RELIEVED	☐ CONTENT
☐ ANXIOUS	☐ FREE	☐ _____
☐ ANGRY	☐ _____	☐ _____
☐ _____	☐ _____	☐ _____
☐ _____	☐ _____	☐ _____

THIS WAS JUST WHAT I NEEDED BECAUSE...

....

....

....

....

....

....

....

....

....

FEEL-GOOD IDEAS!

Take yourself on a date! Go to a museum, to a movie, out to dinner, or anywhere else you want to go. You, your needs, and your self-care preferences are the priorities, so think about which areas of self-care you need more focus on and make it happen.

MY AWESOME NOTES!

....

....

....

....

....

....

....

....

....

....

....

....

TODAY I CHOSE THIS TYPE OF SELF-CARE:

☐ EMOTIONAL

☐ MENTAL

☐ PHYSICAL

☐ PRACTICAL

☐ SOCIAL

☐ SPIRITUAL

Date: ....

Today's self-care
activity: ....

....

....

....

....

....

....

Choose You check-in...how did I feel?

BEFORE:

☐ CALM
☐ CHEERFUL
☐ IN CONTROL
☐ STRESSED
☐ DISTRACTED
☐ EMOTIONAL
☐ OVERWHELMED
☐ ANXIOUS
☐ ANGRY
☐ _____
☐ _____

DURING:

☐ RELAXED
☐ AWESOME
☐ STRONG
☐ ENERGIZED
☐ HAPPY
☐ SURPRISED
☐ RELIEVED
☐ FREE
☐ _____
☐ _____
☐ _____

AFTER:

☐ HOPEFUL
☐ CONFIDENT
☐ PROUD
☐ PEACEFUL
☐ GROUNDED
☐ FOCUSED
☐ CONTENT
☐ _____
☐ _____
☐ _____
☐ _____

THIS WAS JUST WHAT I NEEDED BECAUSE...

....

....

....

....

....

....

....

....

KEEP IT GOING!

It's normal to have at least one friend whose self-care activities exceed what you're able to do. Rather than feel jealous or wish that your self-care could be "better," focus on being appreciative for the time you have and what you *are* able to do.

MY AWESOME NOTES!

....

....

....

....

....

....

....

....

....

....

....

TODAY I CHOSE THIS TYPE OF SELF-CARE:

☐ EMOTIONAL

☐ MENTAL

☐ PHYSICAL

☐ PRACTICAL

☐ SOCIAL

☐ SPIRITUAL

DATE: ....

TODAY'S SELF−CARE ACTIVITY: ....

....

....

....

....

....

....

☐ MAKE THIS A REGULAR ACTIVITY

☐ THIS IS GREAT FOR SPECIAL OCCASIONS

☐ GIVE THIS ANOTHER TRY ON A DIFFERENT DAY

☐ THIS ISN'T FOR ME

CHOOSE YOU CHECK−IN...HOW DID I FEEL?

BEFORE:

☐ CALM
☐ CHEERFUL
☐ IN CONTROL
☐ STRESSED
☐ DISTRACTED
☐ EMOTIONAL
☐ OVERWHELMED
☐ ANXIOUS
☐ ANGRY
☐ _____
☐ _____

DURING:

☐ RELAXED
☐ AWESOME
☐ STRONG
☐ ENERGIZED
☐ HAPPY
☐ SURPRISED
☐ RELIEVED
☐ FREE
☐ _____
☐ _____

AFTER:

☐ HOPEFUL
☐ CONFIDENT
☐ PROUD
☐ PEACEFUL
☐ GROUNDED
☐ FOCUSED
☐ CONTENT
☐ _____
☐ _____
☐ _____

This was just what I needed because...

FEEL-GOOD IDEAS!

Read something related to self-care for inspiration and motivation to keep up the habit. Buy or check out a book at the library or find a blog post or article to read. Reading is mental and emotional self-care; reading *about* self-care is a double dose!

My awesome notes!

TODAY I CHOSE THIS TYPE OF SELF-CARE:

☐ EMOTIONAL

☐ MENTAL

☐ PHYSICAL

☐ PRACTICAL

☐ SOCIAL

☐ SPIRITUAL

DATE: ....

TODAY'S SELF-CARE ACTIVITY: ....

....

....

....

....

....

....

TODAY'S —— TAKEAWAY!

- ☐ MAKE THIS A REGULAR ACTIVITY
- ☐ THIS IS GREAT FOR SPECIAL OCCASIONS
- ☐ GIVE THIS ANOTHER TRY ON A DIFFERENT DAY
- ☐ THIS ISN'T FOR ME

CHOOSE YOU CHECK-IN...HOW DID I FEEL?

BEFORE:	DURING:	AFTER:
☐ CALM	☐ RELAXED	☐ HOPEFUL
☐ CHEERFUL	☐ AWESOME	☐ CONFIDENT
☐ IN CONTROL	☐ STRONG	☐ PROUD
☐ STRESSED	☐ ENERGIZED	☐ PEACEFUL
☐ DISTRACTED	☐ HAPPY	☐ GROUNDED
☐ EMOTIONAL	☐ SURPRISED	☐ FOCUSED
☐ OVERWHELMED	☐ RELIEVED	☐ CONTENT
☐ ANXIOUS	☐ FREE	☐ _____
☐ ANGRY	☐ _____	☐ _____
☐ _____	☐ _____	☐ _____
☐ _____	☐ _____	☐ _____

THIS WAS JUST WHAT I NEEDED BECAUSE...

STAY INSPIRED!

"The key to happiness is being happy by yourself and for yourself. Happiness comes from within. You have the power to change your own mind-set so that all the negative, horrible thoughts that try to invade your psyche are replaced with happy, positive, wonderful thoughts."

—Ellen DeGeneres, comedian

MY AWESOME NOTES!

TODAY I CHOSE THIS TYPE OF SELF-CARE:

☐ EMOTIONAL

☐ MENTAL

☐ PHYSICAL

☐ PRACTICAL

☐ SOCIAL

☐ SPIRITUAL

DATE: ....

TODAY'S SELF-CARE ACTIVITY: ....

....

....

....

....

....

....

☐ MAKE THIS A REGULAR ACTIVITY

☐ THIS IS GREAT FOR SPECIAL OCCASIONS

☐ GIVE THIS ANOTHER TRY ON A DIFFERENT DAY

☐ THIS ISN'T FOR ME

CHOOSE YOU CHECK-IN...HOW DID I FEEL?

BEFORE:

☐ CALM

☐ CHEERFUL

☐ IN CONTROL

☐ STRESSED

☐ DISTRACTED

☐ EMOTIONAL

☐ OVERWHELMED

☐ ANXIOUS

☐ ANGRY

☐ _____

☐ _____

DURING:

☐ RELAXED

☐ AWESOME

☐ STRONG

☐ ENERGIZED

☐ HAPPY

☐ SURPRISED

☐ RELIEVED

☐ FREE

☐ _____

☐ _____

☐ _____

AFTER:

☐ HOPEFUL

☐ CONFIDENT

☐ PROUD

☐ PEACEFUL

☐ GROUNDED

☐ FOCUSED

☐ CONTENT

☐ _____

☐ _____

☐ _____

THIS WAS JUST WHAT I NEEDED BECAUSE...

....

....

....

....

....

....

....

....

FEEL-GOOD IDEAS!

Go through your closet and practice practical and emotional self-care by getting rid of anything that makes you feel less than your best. Now you can have a cleaner closet *and* bless someone else by donating the clothes you no longer need.

MY AWESOME NOTES!

....

....

....

....

....

....

....

....

....

....

TODAY I CHOSE THIS TYPE OF SELF-CARE:

☐ EMOTIONAL

☐ MENTAL

☐ PHYSICAL

☐ PRACTICAL

☐ SOCIAL

☐ SPIRITUAL

DATE: ....

TODAY'S SELF—CARE ACTIVITY: ....

....

....

....

....

....

....

....

TODAY'S TAKEAWAY!

☐ **MAKE THIS A REGULAR ACTIVITY**

☐ **THIS IS GREAT FOR SPECIAL OCCASIONS**

☐ **GIVE THIS ANOTHER TRY ON A DIFFERENT DAY**

☐ **THIS ISN'T FOR ME**

CHOOSE YOU CHECK-IN...HOW DID I FEEL?

BEFORE:	DURING:	AFTER:
☐ CALM	☐ RELAXED	☐ HOPEFUL
☐ CHEERFUL	☐ AWESOME	☐ CONFIDENT
☐ IN CONTROL	☐ STRONG	☐ PROUD
☐ STRESSED	☐ ENERGIZED	☐ PEACEFUL
☐ DISTRACTED	☐ HAPPY	☐ GROUNDED
☐ EMOTIONAL	☐ SURPRISED	☐ FOCUSED
☐ OVERWHELMED	☐ RELIEVED	☐ CONTENT
☐ ANXIOUS	☐ FREE	☐ _____
☐ ANGRY	☐ _____	☐ _____
☐ _____	☐ _____	☐ _____
☐ _____	☐ _____	☐ _____

THIS WAS JUST WHAT I NEEDED BECAUSE...

....

....

....

....

....

....

....

....

....

KEEP IT GOING!

Quick self-care can still be effective self-care! When you feel like your time is limited, make a choice to fit in an activity that takes five minutes or less, like reading a chapter in a book or listening to a brief guided meditation.

MY AWESOME NOTES!

....

....

....

....

....

....

....

....

....

....

....

....

TODAY I CHOSE THIS TYPE OF SELF—CARE:

☐ EMOTIONAL

☐ MENTAL

☐ PHYSICAL

☐ PRACTICAL

☐ SOCIAL

☐ SPIRITUAL

Date: ....

Today's self-care activity: ....

....

....

....

....

....

....

TODAY'S —— —— TAKEAWAY!

☐ MAKE THIS A REGULAR ACTIVITY

☐ THIS IS GREAT FOR SPECIAL OCCASIONS

☐ GIVE THIS ANOTHER TRY ON A DIFFERENT DAY

☐ THIS ISN'T FOR ME

CHOOSE YOU CHECK-IN... HOW DID I FEEL?

BEFORE:

☐ CALM
☐ CHEERFUL
☐ IN CONTROL
☐ STRESSED
☐ DISTRACTED
☐ EMOTIONAL
☐ OVERWHELMED
☐ ANXIOUS
☐ ANGRY
☐ _____
☐ _____

DURING:

☐ RELAXED
☐ AWESOME
☐ STRONG
☐ ENERGIZED
☐ HAPPY
☐ SURPRISED
☐ RELIEVED
☐ FREE
☐ _____
☐ _____

AFTER:

☐ HOPEFUL
☐ CONFIDENT
☐ PROUD
☐ PEACEFUL
☐ GROUNDED
☐ FOCUSED
☐ CONTENT
☐ _____
☐ _____
☐ _____

THIS WAS JUST WHAT I NEEDED BECAUSE...

....
....
....
....
....
....
....
....

MY AWESOME NOTES!

....
....
....
....
....
....
....
....
....
....

TODAY I CHOSE THIS TYPE OF SELF-CARE:

☐ EMOTIONAL

☐ MENTAL

☐ PHYSICAL

☐ PRACTICAL

☐ SOCIAL

☐ SPIRITUAL

Date:

Today's self-care activity:

Choose You check-in...How did I feel?

BEFORE:	DURING:	AFTER:
☐ CALM	☐ RELAXED	☐ HOPEFUL
☐ CHEERFUL	☐ AWESOME	☐ CONFIDENT
☐ IN CONTROL	☐ STRONG	☐ PROUD
☐ STRESSED	☐ ENERGIZED	☐ PEACEFUL
☐ DISTRACTED	☐ HAPPY	☐ GROUNDED
☐ EMOTIONAL	☐ SURPRISED	☐ FOCUSED
☐ OVERWHELMED	☐ RELIEVED	☐ CONTENT
☐ ANXIOUS	☐ FREE	☐ _____
☐ ANGRY	☐ _____	☐ _____
☐ _____	☐ _____	☐ _____
☐ _____	☐ _____	

THIS WAS JUST WHAT I NEEDED BECAUSE...

....
....
....
....
....
....
....
....
....

KEEP IT GOING!

Remember that self-care should help take care of your body, mind, and spirit. As you practice your self-care, make sure you do activities that hit on all three. (Not necessarily at the same time!) Look back at the previous pages in your journal to see which area you might need to spend more time on.

MY AWESOME NOTES!

....
....
....
....
....
....
....
....
....
....
....

TODAY I CHOSE THIS TYPE OF SELF-CARE:

☐ EMOTIONAL

☐ MENTAL

☐ PHYSICAL

☐ PRACTICAL

☐ SOCIAL

☐ SPIRITUAL

DATE: ....

TODAY'S SELF-CARE ACTIVITY: ....

....

....

....

....

....

....

☐ MAKE THIS A REGULAR ACTIVITY

☐ THIS IS GREAT FOR SPECIAL OCCASIONS

☐ GIVE THIS ANOTHER TRY ON A DIFFERENT DAY

☐ THIS ISN'T FOR ME

CHOOSE YOU CHECK-IN...HOW DID I FEEL?

BEFORE:	DURING:	AFTER:
☐ CALM	☐ RELAXED	☐ HOPEFUL
☐ CHEERFUL	☐ AWESOME	☐ CONFIDENT
☐ IN CONTROL	☐ STRONG	☐ PROUD
☐ STRESSED	☐ ENERGIZED	☐ PEACEFUL
☐ DISTRACTED	☐ HAPPY	☐ GROUNDED
☐ EMOTIONAL	☐ SURPRISED	☐ FOCUSED
☐ OVERWHELMED	☐ RELIEVED	☐ CONTENT
☐ ANXIOUS	☐ FREE	☐ _____
☐ ANGRY	☐ _____	☐ _____
☐ _____	☐ _____	☐ _____
☐ _____	☐ _____	☐ _____

THIS WAS JUST WHAT I NEEDED BECAUSE...

....
....
....
....
....
....
....
....

FEEL-GOOD IDEAS! Today, make time to connect with someone you care about. Pick up the phone and call (not text!) a friend or loved one or ask someone to meet up for a visit. Get those social needs met!

MY AWESOME NOTES!

....
....
....
....
....
....
....
....
....
....
....

TODAY I CHOSE THIS TYPE OF SELF-CARE:

☐ **EMOTIONAL**

☐ **MENTAL**

☐ **PHYSICAL**

☐ **PRACTICAL**

☐ **SOCIAL**

☐ **SPIRITUAL**

DATE: ....

TODAY'S SELF-CARE ACTIVITY: ....

....

....

....

....

....

....

CHOOSE YOU CHECK-IN...HOW DID I FEEL?

BEFORE:	DURING:	AFTER:
☐ CALM	☐ RELAXED	☐ HOPEFUL
☐ CHEERFUL	☐ AWESOME	☐ CONFIDENT
☐ IN CONTROL	☐ STRONG	☐ PROUD
☐ STRESSED	☐ ENERGIZED	☐ PEACEFUL
☐ DISTRACTED	☐ HAPPY	☐ GROUNDED
☐ EMOTIONAL	☐ SURPRISED	☐ FOCUSED
☐ OVERWHELMED	☐ RELIEVED	☐ CONTENT
☐ ANXIOUS	☐ FREE	☐ _____
☐ ANGRY	☐ _____	☐ _____
☐ _____	☐ _____	☐ _____
☐ _____	☐ _____	☐ _____

THIS WAS JUST WHAT I NEEDED BECAUSE...

....

....

....

....

....

....

....

....

....

KEEP IT GOING! Give yourself grace when it comes to self-care. Be kind to yourself in your efforts to take care of yourself, and realize that you probably won't *always* follow through with what you've started. Learn from that and move on to restart your self-care momentum.

MY AWESOME NOTES!

....

....

....

....

....

....

....

....

....

....

....

....

TODAY I CHOSE THIS TYPE OF SELF-CARE:

□ EMOTIONAL

□ MENTAL

□ PHYSICAL

□ PRACTICAL

□ SOCIAL

□ SPIRITUAL

Date: ....

Today's self-care activity: ....

....

....

....

....

....

....

TODAY'S — —TAKEAWAY!

- ☐ MAKE THIS A REGULAR ACTIVITY
- ☐ THIS IS GREAT FOR SPECIAL OCCASIONS
- ☐ GIVE THIS ANOTHER TRY ON A DIFFERENT DAY
- ☐ THIS ISN'T FOR ME

Choose You check-in... HOW DID I FEEL?

BEFORE:	DURING:	AFTER:
☐ CALM	☐ RELAXED	☐ HOPEFUL
☐ CHEERFUL	☐ AWESOME	☐ CONFIDENT
☐ IN CONTROL	☐ STRONG	☐ PROUD
☐ STRESSED	☐ ENERGIZED	☐ PEACEFUL
☐ DISTRACTED	☐ HAPPY	☐ GROUNDED
☐ EMOTIONAL	☐ SURPRISED	☐ FOCUSED
☐ OVERWHELMED	☐ RELIEVED	☐ CONTENT
☐ ANXIOUS	☐ FREE	☐ _____
☐ ANGRY	☐ _____	☐ _____
☐ _____	☐ _____	☐ _____
☐ _____	☐ _____	☐ _____

THIS WAS JUST WHAT I NEEDED BECAUSE...

....
....
....
....
....
....
....

MY AWESOME NOTES!

....
....
....
....
....
....
....
....
....

TODAY I CHOSE THIS TYPE OF SELF-CARE:

☐ EMOTIONAL

☐ MENTAL

☐ PHYSICAL

☐ PRACTICAL

☐ SOCIAL

☐ SPIRITUAL

*D*ATE: ....

*T*ODAY'S SELF-CARE
ACTIVITY: ....

....

....

....

....

....

....

- ☐ MAKE THIS A REGULAR ACTIVITY
- ☐ THIS IS GREAT FOR SPECIAL OCCASIONS
- ☐ GIVE THIS ANOTHER TRY ON A DIFFERENT DAY
- ☐ THIS ISN'T FOR ME

*C*HOOSE *Y*OU CHECK-IN...HOW DID I FEEL?

BEFORE:

- ☐ CALM
- ☐ CHEERFUL
- ☐ IN CONTROL
- ☐ STRESSED
- ☐ DISTRACTED
- ☐ EMOTIONAL
- ☐ OVERWHELMED
- ☐ ANXIOUS
- ☐ ANGRY
- ☐ _____
- ☐ _____

DURING:

- ☐ RELAXED
- ☐ AWESOME
- ☐ STRONG
- ☐ ENERGIZED
- ☐ HAPPY
- ☐ SURPRISED
- ☐ RELIEVED
- ☐ FREE
- ☐ _____
- ☐ _____
- ☐ _____

AFTER:

- ☐ HOPEFUL
- ☐ CONFIDENT
- ☐ PROUD
- ☐ PEACEFUL
- ☐ GROUNDED
- ☐ FOCUSED
- ☐ CONTENT
- ☐ _____
- ☐ _____
- ☐ _____

THIS WAS JUST WHAT I NEEDED BECAUSE...

....

....

....

....

....

....

....

....

FEEL-GOOD IDEAS!

Create a system or routine for something that is more stressful than it needs to be. For example, make lunchtime easier on yourself. Plan and prepare for the week ahead each weekend to give yourself healthy meals. Routines related to practical needs create more simplicity and less stress.

MY AWESOME NOTES!

....

....

....

....

....

....

....

....

....

....

TODAY I CHOSE THIS TYPE OF SELF-CARE:

☐ EMOTIONAL

☐ MENTAL

☐ PHYSICAL

☐ PRACTICAL

☐ SOCIAL

☐ SPIRITUAL

Date: ....

Today's self-care activity: ....

....
....
....
....
....
....

Choose You check-in...How did I feel?

BEFORE:	DURING:	AFTER:
☐ CALM	☐ RELAXED	☐ HOPEFUL
☐ CHEERFUL	☐ AWESOME	☐ CONFIDENT
☐ IN CONTROL	☐ STRONG	☐ PROUD
☐ STRESSED	☐ ENERGIZED	☐ PEACEFUL
☐ DISTRACTED	☐ HAPPY	☐ GROUNDED
☐ EMOTIONAL	☐ SURPRISED	☐ FOCUSED
☐ OVERWHELMED	☐ RELIEVED	☐ CONTENT
☐ ANXIOUS	☐ FREE	☐ _____
☐ ANGRY	☐ _____	☐ _____
☐ _____	☐ _____	☐ _____
☐ _____	☐ _____	☐ _____

THIS WAS JUST WHAT I NEEDED BECAUSE...

....

....

....

....

....

....

....

....

....

....

KEEP IT GOING!

Sometimes we try new things as part of taking care of ourselves, and it's easy for judgment to take over. It doesn't matter how flexible you are, how well you can do the activity, or that you've never done it before. You're doing it! That's the important part.

MY AWESOME NOTES!

....

....

....

....

....

....

....

....

....

....

....

TODAY I CHOSE THIS TYPE OF SELF-CARE:

- ☐ EMOTIONAL
- ☐ MENTAL
- ☐ PHYSICAL
- ☐ PRACTICAL
- ☐ SOCIAL
- ☐ SPIRITUAL

DATE: ....

TODAY'S SELF-CARE ACTIVITY: ....

....
....
....
....
....
....
....

☐ **MAKE THIS A REGULAR ACTIVITY**

☐ **THIS IS GREAT FOR SPECIAL OCCASIONS**

☐ **GIVE THIS ANOTHER TRY ON A DIFFERENT DAY**

☐ **THIS ISN'T FOR ME**

CHOOSE YOU CHECK-IN...HOW DID I FEEL?

BEFORE:

☐ CALM
☐ CHEERFUL
☐ IN CONTROL
☐ STRESSED
☐ DISTRACTED
☐ EMOTIONAL
☐ OVERWHELMED
☐ ANXIOUS
☐ ANGRY
☐ _____
☐ _____

DURING:

☐ RELAXED
☐ AWESOME
☐ STRONG
☐ ENERGIZED
☐ HAPPY
☐ SURPRISED
☐ RELIEVED
☐ FREE
☐ _____
☐ _____
☐ _____

AFTER:

☐ HOPEFUL
☐ CONFIDENT
☐ PROUD
☐ PEACEFUL
☐ GROUNDED
☐ FOCUSED
☐ CONTENT
☐ _____
☐ _____
☐ _____

THIS WAS JUST WHAT I NEEDED BECAUSE...

....

....

....

....

....

....

....

....

FEEL–GOOD IDEAS!

Meet your spiritual needs, whatever those are. Take the time to reflect on what's important to fill you up in a spiritual or religious way, then build those activities into your schedule as much as you need.

MY AWESOME NOTES!

....

....

....

....

....

....

....

....

....

....

....

TODAY I CHOSE THIS TYPE OF SELF–CARE:

- ☐ EMOTIONAL
- ☐ MENTAL
- ☐ PHYSICAL
- ☐ PRACTICAL
- ☐ SOCIAL
- ☐ SPIRITUAL

Date: ....

Today's self-care
activity: ....

....
....
....
....
....
....

Choose You check-in... HOW DID I FEEL?

BEFORE:	DURING:	AFTER:
☐ CALM	☐ RELAXED	☐ HOPEFUL
☐ CHEERFUL	☐ AWESOME	☐ CONFIDENT
☐ IN CONTROL	☐ STRONG	☐ PROUD
☐ STRESSED	☐ ENERGIZED	☐ PEACEFUL
☐ DISTRACTED	☐ HAPPY	☐ GROUNDED
☐ EMOTIONAL	☐ SURPRISED	☐ FOCUSED
☐ OVERWHELMED	☐ RELIEVED	☐ CONTENT
☐ ANXIOUS	☐ FREE	☐ _____
☐ ANGRY	☐ _____	☐ _____
☐ _____	☐ _____	☐ _____
☐ _____	☐ _____	☐ _____

THIS WAS JUST WHAT I NEEDED BECAUSE...

STAY INSPIRED!

"Nourishing yourself in a way that helps you blossom in the direction you want to go is attainable, and you are worth the effort."

—Deborah Day, MA, author

MY AWESOME NOTES!

TODAY I CHOSE THIS TYPE OF SELF-CARE:

☐ EMOTIONAL

☐ MENTAL

☐ PHYSICAL

☐ PRACTICAL

☐ SOCIAL

☐ SPIRITUAL

DATE: ....

TODAY'S SELF-CARE ACTIVITY: ....

....

....

....

....

....

....

- ☐ MAKE THIS A REGULAR ACTIVITY
- ☐ THIS IS GREAT FOR SPECIAL OCCASIONS
- ☐ GIVE THIS ANOTHER TRY ON A DIFFERENT DAY
- ☐ THIS ISN'T FOR ME

CHOOSE YOU CHECK-IN...HOW DID I FEEL?

BEFORE:

- ☐ CALM
- ☐ CHEERFUL
- ☐ IN CONTROL
- ☐ STRESSED
- ☐ DISTRACTED
- ☐ EMOTIONAL
- ☐ OVERWHELMED
- ☐ ANXIOUS
- ☐ ANGRY
- ☐ _____
- ☐ _____

DURING:

- ☐ RELAXED
- ☐ AWESOME
- ☐ STRONG
- ☐ ENERGIZED
- ☐ HAPPY
- ☐ SURPRISED
- ☐ RELIEVED
- ☐ FREE
- ☐ _____
- ☐ _____
- ☐ _____

AFTER:

- ☐ HOPEFUL
- ☐ CONFIDENT
- ☐ PROUD
- ☐ PEACEFUL
- ☐ GROUNDED
- ☐ FOCUSED
- ☐ CONTENT
- ☐ _____
- ☐ _____
- ☐ _____

THIS WAS JUST WHAT I NEEDED BECAUSE...

....
....
....
....
....
....
....
....

MY AWESOME NOTES!

....
....
....
....
....
....
....
....
....
....

TODAY I CHOSE THIS TYPE OF SELF-CARE:

☐ EMOTIONAL

☐ MENTAL

☐ PHYSICAL

☐ PRACTICAL

☐ SOCIAL

☐ SPIRITUAL

DATE: ....

TODAY'S SELF—CARE ACTIVITY: ....

....
....
....
....
....
....

CHOOSE YOU CHECK-IN...HOW DID I FEEL?

BEFORE:	DURING:	AFTER:
☐ CALM	☐ RELAXED	☐ HOPEFUL
☐ CHEERFUL	☐ AWESOME	☐ CONFIDENT
☐ IN CONTROL	☐ STRONG	☐ PROUD
☐ STRESSED	☐ ENERGIZED	☐ PEACEFUL
☐ DISTRACTED	☐ HAPPY	☐ GROUNDED
☐ EMOTIONAL	☐ SURPRISED	☐ FOCUSED
☐ OVERWHELMED	☐ RELIEVED	☐ CONTENT
☐ ANXIOUS	☐ FREE	☐ _____
☐ ANGRY	☐ _____	☐ _____
☐ _____	☐ _____	☐ _____
☐ _____	☐ _____	☐ _____

THIS WAS JUST WHAT I NEEDED BECAUSE...

....

....

....

....

....

....

....

....

KEEP IT GOING!

Self-care is an ongoing practice; if you miss a day or two (or more), that's okay. It happens. Figure out what got in the way and keep going. It's important to learn from your successes and struggles to make self-care a regular habit.

MY AWESOME NOTES!

....

....

....

....

....

....

....

....

....

....

....

....

TODAY I CHOSE THIS TYPE OF SELF-CARE:

- ☐ EMOTIONAL
- ☐ MENTAL
- ☐ PHYSICAL
- ☐ PRACTICAL
- ☐ SOCIAL
- ☐ SPIRITUAL

*D*ATE: ....

*T*ODAY'S SELF-CARE
ACTIVITY: ....

....

....

....

....

....

....

TODAY'S
TAKEAWAY!

☐ **MAKE THIS A
REGULAR ACTIVITY**

☐ **THIS IS GREAT
FOR SPECIAL
OCCASIONS**

☐ **GIVE THIS ANOTHER
TRY ON A
DIFFERENT DAY**

☐ **THIS ISN'T FOR ME**

*C*HOOSE *Y*OU CHECK-IN...HOW DID I FEEL?

BEFORE:	DURING:	AFTER:
☐ CALM	☐ RELAXED	☐ HOPEFUL
☐ CHEERFUL	☐ AWESOME	☐ CONFIDENT
☐ IN CONTROL	☐ STRONG	☐ PROUD
☐ STRESSED	☐ ENERGIZED	☐ PEACEFUL
☐ DISTRACTED	☐ HAPPY	☐ GROUNDED
☐ EMOTIONAL	☐ SURPRISED	☐ FOCUSED
☐ OVERWHELMED	☐ RELIEVED	☐ CONTENT
☐ ANXIOUS	☐ FREE	☐ _____
☐ ANGRY	☐ _____	☐ _____
☐ _____	☐ _____	☐ _____
☐ _____	☐ _____	☐ _____

THIS WAS JUST WHAT I NEEDED BECAUSE...

FEEL-GOOD IDEAS!

Do an at-home spa day, alone or with friends. Soak your feet in the tub with Epsom salts, paint your nails, and give yourself a facial. Listen to great music, burn a scented candle, or diffuse scented oils. You're taking care of lots of types of self-care needs here, so enjoy!

MY AWESOME NOTES!

TODAY I CHOSE THIS TYPE OF SELF-CARE:

☐ EMOTIONAL

☐ MENTAL

☐ PHYSICAL

☐ PRACTICAL

☐ SOCIAL

☐ SPIRITUAL

DATE: ....

TODAY'S SELF-CARE
ACTIVITY: ....

....

....

....

....

....

....

TODAY'S——
——*TAKEAWAY!*

- ☐ MAKE THIS A REGULAR ACTIVITY
- ☐ THIS IS GREAT FOR SPECIAL OCCASIONS
- ☐ GIVE THIS ANOTHER TRY ON A DIFFERENT DAY
- ☐ THIS ISN'T FOR ME

CHOOSE YOU CHECK-IN... HOW DID I FEEL?

BEFORE:	DURING:	AFTER:
☐ CALM	☐ RELAXED	☐ HOPEFUL
☐ CHEERFUL	☐ AWESOME	☐ CONFIDENT
☐ IN CONTROL	☐ STRONG	☐ PROUD
☐ STRESSED	☐ ENERGIZED	☐ PEACEFUL
☐ DISTRACTED	☐ HAPPY	☐ GROUNDED
☐ EMOTIONAL	☐ SURPRISED	☐ FOCUSED
☐ OVERWHELMED	☐ RELIEVED	☐ CONTENT
☐ ANXIOUS	☐ FREE	☐ _____
☐ ANGRY	☐ _____	☐ _____
☐ _____	☐ _____	☐ _____
☐ _____	☐ _____	☐ _____

THIS WAS JUST WHAT I NEEDED BECAUSE...

MY AWESOME NOTES!

TODAY I CHOSE THIS TYPE OF SELF-CARE:

☐ EMOTIONAL

☐ MENTAL

☐ PHYSICAL

☐ PRACTICAL

☐ SOCIAL

☐ SPIRITUAL

*D*ATE: ....

*T*ODAY'S SELF—CARE
ACTIVITY: ....

....

....

....

....

....

....

🌿 *TODAY'S TAKEAWAY!* 🌿

☐ **MAKE THIS A REGULAR ACTIVITY**

☐ **THIS IS GREAT FOR SPECIAL OCCASIONS**

☐ **GIVE THIS ANOTHER TRY ON A DIFFERENT DAY**

☐ **THIS ISN'T FOR ME**

*C*HOOSE *Y*OU CHECK-IN...HOW DID I FEEL?

BEFORE:	*DURING:*	*AFTER:*
☐ CALM	☐ RELAXED	☐ HOPEFUL
☐ CHEERFUL	☐ AWESOME	☐ CONFIDENT
☐ IN CONTROL	☐ STRONG	☐ PROUD
☐ STRESSED	☐ ENERGIZED	☐ PEACEFUL
☐ DISTRACTED	☐ HAPPY	☐ GROUNDED
☐ EMOTIONAL	☐ SURPRISED	☐ FOCUSED
☐ OVERWHELMED	☐ RELIEVED	☐ CONTENT
☐ ANXIOUS	☐ FREE	☐ _____
☐ ANGRY	☐ _____	☐ _____
☐ _____	☐ _____	☐ _____
☐ _____	☐ _____	

THIS WAS JUST WHAT I NEEDED BECAUSE...

....

....

....

....

....

....

....

....

MY AWESOME NOTES!

....

....

....

....

....

....

....

....

....

....

KEEP IT GOING!
Self-care isn't just doing things for *yourself*; it's also doing things that help you feel more full and complete. So self-care can be helping others or taking care of tasks for your family that help you feel more organized and in control.

TODAY I CHOSE THIS TYPE OF SELF–CARE:

☐ EMOTIONAL

☐ MENTAL

☐ PHYSICAL

☐ PRACTICAL

☐ SOCIAL

☐ SPIRITUAL

ABOUT THE AUTHOR

For the last decade, as a mental skills coach, Sara Robinson has helped individuals change the way they think and feel to create positive behavioral changes. Sara regularly speaks about the importance of balance and self-care and has been a guest on *The SuperMum Podcast* and *The Mom Inspired Show* and a speaker for the Mom Project Summit 2017. Her blog, *Get Mom Balanced* (GetMomBalanced.com), aims to support busy working moms to find balance and time for self-care and help moms develop the mental skills that they need to thrive. She has regularly contributed to online publications, including *RunSmart Online* and the *LPGA Women's Network* blog. Sara has a master's degree in sport psychology.